HORSE TRAINING

Beginner's Guide to Successfully Understanding and Training Your Horse

(A Positive Approach to Training Equines and Understanding Them and Groundwork Training for Horses)

Rodger Benning

Published By Rodger Benning

Rodger Benning

All Rights Reserved

Horse Training: Beginner's Guide to Successfully Understanding and Training Your Horse (A Positive Approach to Training Equines and Understanding Them and Groundwork Training for Horses)

ISBN 978-1-77485-405-1

All rights reserved. No part of this guide may be reproduced in any form without permission in writing from the publisher except in the case of brief quotations embodied in critical articles or reviews.

Legal & Disclaimer

The information contained in this book is not designed to replace or take the place of any form of medicine or professional medical advice. The information in this book has been provided for educational and entertainment purposes only.

The information contained in this book has been compiled from sources deemed reliable, and it is accurate to the best of the Author's knowledge; however, the Author cannot guarantee its accuracy and validity and cannot be held liable for any errors or omissions. Changes are periodically made to this book. You must consult your doctor or get professional medical advice before using any of the suggested remedies, techniques, or information in this book.

Upon using the information contained in this book, you agree to hold harmless the Author from and against any damages, costs, and expenses, including any legal fees potentially resulting from the application of any of the information provided by this guide. This disclaimer applies to any damages or injury caused by the use and application, whether directly or indirectly, of any advice or information presented, whether for breach of contract, tort, negligence, personal injury, criminal intent, or under any other cause of action.

You agree to accept all risks of using the information presented inside this book. You need to consult a professional medical practitioner in order to ensure you are both able and healthy enough to participate in this program.

TABLE OF CONTENTS

INTRODUCTION 1

CHAPTER 1: EXPLAINS HOW TO BUY HORSES HORSE 7

CHAPTER 2: CHOOSING THE BEST BREED 12

CHAPTER 3: BEHAVIORAL HORSE TRAINING 32

CHAPTER 4: GLOBAL HORSE KEEPING AND RIDING 43

CHAPTER 5: DIFFERENT TYPES OF HORSE TRAINING 66

CHAPTER 6: SOCIALIZING YOUR HORSE 80

CHAPTER 7: HOW CAN I IMPROVE MY TROT POSITION? . 97

CHAPTER 8: HORSE STALL AND PADDOCK 105

CHAPTER 9: UNDERSTANDING YOUR HORSE 124

CHAPTER 10: FIGHT OR FLIGHT 132

CHAPTER 11: HORSE BREEDING 151

CHAPTER 12: A DIFFERENT METHOD TO GET YOUR HORSE INTO THE TRAILER 175

CONCLUSION 183

Introduction

Horses are beautiful animals that can be utilized in a range of applications because of their inherent traits. They are employed in numerous sports, riding for recreation and also a range of other applications. It is because of the need for use that horses are typically trained. Whatever way you are planning to utilize horses, it is crucial to understand the basics of how you can train it to do it correctly and get the desired outcomes. It is a general rule that every horse exercise tends to be focused on getting to a certain objective. Be sure to have set goals.

What exactly is Horse Training?

Before we can discuss the reasons horse trainers are needed, it's crucial to have an knowledge of what exactly horse training actually is. Horse training is the repetition of different exercises to become familiar with the training from a physical as well as mental perspective. All horse training exercises are designed to assist the horse to develop some kind of physical fitness and stamina. As a trainer of horses or owner, it is essential to be aware of the distinction between physical and mental horse training. This will assist you to understand why training routines are diverse and numerous.

Horse Training Goals

As previously mentioned the horse's training should not be performed randomly and should be designed to achieve certain goals. In essence, training for horses can be designed to help horses develop different habits. This includes the entire training process that is designed to help the horse improve their understanding of specific gestures and signs. This could include teaching the horse to recognize the manner in which the trainer or owner wants to take it off or onto the trailer. It could also involve instructing the horse to stay still while the saddle is put in its place, and then the rider is able to mount it.

However it is possible to use horse training utilized to increase the physical strength of horses. These training exercises are designed to strengthening the horse's muscles in order to strengthen it and make it more able, based on the purpose of the horse. These exercises are designed to help horses run faster, increase the endurance of its muscles and leap higher. These are usually the most well-known horse-training exercises and are the first thing that comes to mind when you hear of horse-training.

Motives behind Horse Training

A crucial aspect of understanding the best way to teach a horse is knowing the reasons why horse owners need training. What is the reason why owners of horses spend an enormous amount of money and time making sure their horses are being trained every day? The answer to this question will assist in helping you understand the necessity of training your horse at all times and the importance of executing it with perfection in improving the overall quality of your horse's life.

Making them easy to Ride

Many owners of horses today typically use them to ride. It could be to relax or for racing at high speed. It is vital to understand that, even though horses have been domesticated for a long time however, the fact that they are born with temperaments that differ means they need to be taught over and over again in order in a position to withstand humans and riding. It is essential to understand that riding doesn't just encompass the ability to mount and saddle the horse as well as the understanding required. The horse has to be able to recognize the instructions of the rider, and thus allow riding to be safe and possible.

Improve Performance

Horse training involves performing numerous exercises to strengthen the horse and increase its performance. Horses are used in jumping and racing as well in order to improve their performance for these tasks, it's important to ensure the horse is in top physical fitness. The muscles required for these activities have to be strong and strong enough. There are many diverse horse-related actions and exercises that aim to improve the fitness level of horses. In regular training sessions, it is essential to be aware of the variety of exercises that are designed to increase the physical fitness of the horse within the field of operations.

Reduce the risk of injury

Horses are extremely muscular creatures. Their entire body is composed from a set of muscles that are attached to their bones. The front legs of their bodies aren't directly linked to their skeletons, but are connected indirectly via a network of muscles. The feet serve as secondary organs of the heart which pump blood into and out in order to ensure blood circulation issues. Regular exercise helps keep the horse well and safe from injuries throughout the day. This is particularly true for horses that aren't frequently used in physical demanding tasks. the absence of regular exercise in their stable could result in feet swelling due to the lack of blood circulation. This can be avoided with regular training exercises.

Chapter 1: Explains How To Buy Horses Horse

If you've not yet completed the purchase of an animal, here's something you should be aware of. A veterinarian should accompany you to inspect the horse prior to making the purchase. When the vet examines the horse, let him to share with you about what he learns concerning the horse. You'll be able to ask the veterinarian any questions about the horse. If the vet does not believe that the horse is suitable for you, pay attention to him when he suggests that you do not purchase the horse.

If the horse you're looking at has a certain temperament, a particular type of training or lack of it and he is aware of it, the horse's owner could be having problems with the horse in the future and may recommend that you not purchase this particular horse.

If you bring a vet along on your trip to inspect horses, you will not only be paying for a health check for horses, but also to learn about the knowledge of the veterinarian to horses. Some people may think it's not the job of the vet to find the right horse for you. But, in reality, either you or the animal you purchase or do not purchase are better off. If you decide to have a veterinarian accompany you to evaluate the health of a horse, it's best to be attentive to him. He may tell you, if you decide to purchase a particular horse, that it will require an experienced trainer.

A lot of vendors will appear when the vet examines the horse. However they prefer if they don't speak to the horse during the exam. The person you choose to visit could alter your perceptions, but do nothing to boost your confidence.

The vet will also examine your horse to determine if it has any health issues. This can prevent the purchase of the horse that has an ongoing issue that could hinder the horse's ability to perform in the way you want him to do. If you are purchasing the horse for riding and ride, you do not want to be saddled with a horse who's legs cannot support the burden of a rider or is spending the majority part of time and money at the vet.

If the horse is suffering from an existing ailment that you are aware about, and ask the assistance of a vet to examine it, the vet might not accept the request or notify you of any issues associated with the issue before proceeding to a different issue. Veterinarians adhere to professional ethics and typically they will not discuss horses belonging to an existing client because of conflicts of interest.

When it comes to a vet's examination, a lot of people do not want to take someone else's advice, and don't request that the vet perform an examination prior to making the purchase. Horse owners who are new must realize that having a vet examine the horse could save hundreds, if not even hundreds of thousands of dollars by not buying a faulty horse.

Chapter 2: Choosing The Best Breed

There are around 400 different horse breeds that are known to man, each having distinctive characteristics and specificizations. Equestrian contests are a great way to capitalize on the differences between these breeds and take part in a range of sporting events. If you are a owner of a horse it is important to know the distinctions between breeds and their particularizations. In this section we will go over some of the more sought-after breeds of horses, their traits and the way they are used.

Arabian

With its unique arched neck and elegant tail carriage, one can easily recognize the Arabian horse wherever. It was bred by Arab and is among the oldest breeds, whose history extends back to more than four thousand years back. It's versatile and has a strong stamina and is well-known for its endurance racing.

The Arabian is taller than fourteen hands up to sixteen hands (56 inches to 64 inches) and a weight range between 800 and 100 pounds. Arabians are also well-known for their warm and friendly disposition that makes them easy to master and easily attached to human beings. They are extensively used in a variety of equestrian pursuits, including dressage, horse racing showjumping and endurance riding and many others. They are perfect for leisure riding and are often in ranches, even when they are not competing in sporting events.

Thoroughbred

Have you noticed a famous breed of speed and agility utilized in many equestrian competitions? It's very likely that it is a strong and agile Thoroughbred.

Thoroughbred horses have an equally swift and agile stallions, such as horses like the Arabian as well as the Turkoman. They are considered to be one of the "hot-blooded" breed of horses due to its agility, strength and speed. They typically come in grey or dark colors and can range in height from 15.2 hands (62 inches) to 17.0 hands (68 inches).

The most easily identifiable characteristics characteristic of the Thoroughbred include the well-chiseled head and long neck and chest that is deep, a shorter back, lean body and legs that are long. A Thoroughbred is a very energetic and athletic horse that is why it is a great choice for all kinds of equestrian competitions. It's also used to breed horses for riding in other disciplines such as dressage, polo showjumping, and many more.

Appaloosa

Most well-known for its vibrantly colored body The Appaloosa is a well-loved animal throughout North America with a unique history. The breed was first introduced by the Nez-Perce indigenous peoples, it was used for hunting as well as a military animal. Its distinctive spots and color resulted from various breeds crossed over time. Uneven skin color, stripes on hooves and visible white scleras in the eyes are characteristics that define the Appaloosa.

There are a variety of body types that are attributed to the Appaloosa breed due to the breeds in its lineage. The average size is generally between 950 and 1250 kilograms as well as fourteen hands (56 inches) to 15 hands (60 inches) in the height. It is typically employed as a stock horse managing livestock on ranches. It is also used in numerous western riding competitions. Trail riding, leisure riding middle distance and trail riding are just a few of the uses this intelligent and versatile horse is ideal for.

Morgan

The Morgan Horse is a magnificent and unusual horse, with a luxurious carriage, making it ideal for various functions of ceremonial significance and also as coaches. The Morgan Horse was named for the initial owner Justin Morgan, and was used to breed other horses. It is easy to identify an Morgan horse by its smooth walking gait, muscular and refined built, strong hindquarters as well as the high-tail carriage. Morgan breeds are extremely strong and come with a height at 14.1 hands (57 inches) to 15.2 hands (62 inches). The Morgan is widely used in as an English as well as Western riding such as leisure riding and as a competitor in equestrian sports. It is famous for its distinctive temperament, quiet nature as well as its intelligence and boldness.

American Quarter Horse

A quarter-horse is among the most popular breeds of horses in America. It is bred from the Thoroughbred horse, and is extremely adaptable. It is often seen at racehorse events or rodeos due to its ability to travel swiftly over small distances. It is a small but sleek head, strong body structure and hindquarters that are rounded. The average height of a Quarter horse is fourteen hands (56 inches) to 16 hands (64 inches). It is most famous in the field of sports as a sprinter, able to outrun other breeds over one quarter mile or less. It is also widely used as a horse for ranching with its small body. makes it ideal for skilled and technical actions like barrel racing calvesroping, and various western-style riding contests.

Standardbred

The Standardbred horse has the potential to be a multi-faceted North American horse breed whose ability is apparent in harnessing horses and other disciplines of equestrian. Similar to other breeds of horse that are related to it, Standardbred horses have the same ancestry as other stallion breeds, including Thoroughbreds and Morgan and many others. It's quick, agile and has a powerful robust build, slightly more heavy than thoroughbred.

Standardbreds average a size of between 14 hands (56 inches) to 17 hands (68 inches) and weigh anywhere from 800 and 1000 pounds. They are often seen in harness racing events as they are the most fast trotting horse breed that has been identified to mankind. Other applications of the Standardbred include entertainment riding as well as ranch horses, horse shows and, of course they are utilized to breed other horses.

Percheron

The Percheron is an French horse which is the popular breed of horses that is known by the name draft horses. They are distinctive for their robust and durable construction. They've been used as stagecoaches, war horses as well as farm animals because of their strength and bulky build. You can identify the Percheron horse by its massive and bulky legs, wide chest, large size and its docile nature. They are generally referred to as "cold-blooded" due to their calm, calm temperament.

The weight and height of the Percheron vary for different countries and they are extensively employed as workhorses. They are often used in parades, for agricultural reasons and to haul large loads and are crossbred with lighter horses in order to boost stamina, and to produce larger horses for other uses.

Welsh Ponies

Many people know what a pony is at the very least, by their description. They are miniature horses. They are a type of breeds of horses that have the height not more than 14.2 hands (58 inches) at maturity. They are, therefore, smaller than the standard horse, and are ideally the best option for youngsters. They are derived from Wales and include horses from Wales. Arabian as well as Thoroughbred horses being the lineage.

They are available in four varieties identified by their height, with the shorter being just eleven hands (44 inches) and the tallest being 16 hands (64 inches) being the highest. Their fast and smooth movement patterns are often a hallmark of these animals. Welsh ponies are extremely intelligent animals, with a high performance and speed. They are utilized for a variety of reasons, including to work animals, leisure riding, as well as in the equestrian sport competition. They excel in endurance racing, dressage, and driving.

Tennessee Walking Horse

The gaited breed is also called The Tennessee Walker, this unique horse breed is part of a breed of horses that are commonly referred to by the name gaited breeds. Gaited horses are a distinctive type of horses selected to run easily and with the four beat rhythm. Their natural gait is ideal for riders over the age of 40 or those who want a smooth ride.

Tennessee Walker Tennessee Walker is an elegant and robust animal that has range that ranges from 14.3 hands (59 inches) to

17 hands (68 inches) and the weight ranges from 1000 up to 1200 pounds. They are famous due to their tranquil nature and their ability to run. They are frequently employed in trails riding competitions, and also for pleasure riding.

Hanoverian

The Hanoverian horse is in the class of "warm-blooded" breeding horses. They are typically created by breeding with a "hot-blooded" breed with the "cold-blooded" horse. Hanoverians are a breed of horse. Hanoverian is a warmblood breed which originated in Germany. It was refined using Thoroughbred blood to improve its speed and be more athletic. The end result was to be an absolute success.

The Hanoverian breed is elegant, robust and athletic The Hanoverian breed has the potential to be a flexible, energetic horse that has a relaxing environment. It was once used by the military and also as an instructor horse. Nowadays, it is an extremely sought-after and extensively used sports horses since it has medals in every Equestrian Olympic sports. The height range of the Hanoverian breed ranges from 15.3 hands (63 inches) to 17.2 hands (70 inches). It is primarily used as a sport animal, however it can also be ridden to enjoy pleasure.

Mustang

Mustangs are horses that they are most likely to see out in nature. They are free-ranging horses introduced in North America by the Spanish. They are easily identifiable by their short, but strong frame, broad head and small muzzle. The standard Mustang is approximately fourteen hands (56 inches) up to fifteen hands (60 inches). They are renowned by their strength, endurance and their sturdiness. They are utilized in horse race events as well as trails riding, pleasure riding, and as farm animals.

American Paint Horse

A major thing you'll observe concerning one of the first things you will notice about American Paint Horse is its vibrant and vivid coat. Each paint horse has distinct white color as well as a different color for horses. The lineage could be traced to Thoroughbred as well as the Quarter horse breeds.

The typical American Paint Horse has an average height of between 14 and sixteen hands (56 inches to 64 inches) and weighs approximately 950-1200 pounds. A few of its unique characteristics include a strong body and a low centre of gravity that allows for simple maneuvering and strong hindquarters that allow quick motion. It is often employed in western horse shows, such as reining and show jumping.

Haflinger

If you notice a bunch of horses that are a bit short, with a chestnut-colored color They are most likely of the Haflinger horses. Originating originated in Austria and the origins of the Haflinger can be traced to the middle ages. They are strong elegant and stylish, as well as possessing stunning flaxen mare.

The height of the average Haflinger ranges from 13.2 up to 15 hands (54 to 60 inches according to) It is a popular model that is found in chestnut colors. It is a smooth, stride that is able to offer a lively but relaxing ride.

It's ideal for riding under saddle, and is also able to be utilized as a draft or packhorse. The equestrian events that

Haflingers Haflinger involved in are show jumping and vaulting, dressage endurance as well as trail-riding. It can also be used for leisure or therapeutic riding.

American Saddlebred

Another gaited breed is that of the American Saddlebred Horse, is an amazing horse breed that came out of the United States. The lineage of this breed goes back horses with ambling gaits in the British Isles. It has Morgan and Thoroughbred bloodline as part of its ancestral lineage. The Saddlebred is distinguished by the elegant carriage of its lean and muscular frame.

A beautiful and lively horse, the common Saddlebred is a tall horse with an average of 15-17 hands (60 to 68 inches depending on the breed). Beautiful and graceful You can easily spot the Saddlebred due to its exceptional movement and effortless walk. It is ideally utilized for show horses but is also used in other equestrian contests like combined driving, dressage, and saddle riding.

Hackney Horse

It is believed that the Hackney horse breed is a descendent of Britain and was bred as a riding horse with the perfect trot. It is strong and has an elegant frame. It is widely employed as an equestrian due to its elegant and powerful performance.

The average height of a Hackney horse ranges from 14. 2 and 16.2 hands (58 inches to 64 inches) They weigh around 1000 pounds. The high-speed trot as well as the elegant style are typical of it.

It is possible to distinguish the Hackney horse in comparison to other breeds similar to it by its distinctive characteristics, attentive ears, eyes, and naturally high-tail carriage. It is primarily used for carriage horses, and in sports that are competitive, it is used in driving and harness racing events. The powerful hindquarters of the horse to provide a smooth and comfortable stride, which allows for enjoyment and enjoyable riding.

The Best Horse Breed to Choose

Horses are intelligent and emotional creatures that have a personality as well as a brains to their very own. When choosing a horse you should take into account your personal preferences in conjunction with the horse's temperament and personality. The motive for which you intend to train the horse, the knowledge level and experiences with horses should be taken into consideration.

If you're new to horses, you'll require an obedient and patient horse. One that is smart, learns quickly, and is able to create an ambiance that is pleasant. It is the American Quarter Horse, Tennessee Walking Horse, Shire Horse as well as Morgan all fall under this category. They are also great for beginners. horses for kids or ones that are less than 5.5 feet.

Breeds of cold-blooded horses are easy to handle, friendly and affectionate. They tend to be huge and don't have the exuberance that you typically find in sport horses. Their calm nature is ideal for work on farms and in labour. Breeds that are cold-blooded include trotters with coldbloods, Percheron, Belgian Draft and Clydesdale.

Warm-blooded horses are versatile and lively creatures. They're a mix of breeds that are hot-blooded and cold-blooded with the welcoming and inviting ambiance of cold bloods and the power and agility of hot-bloods. It is possible to train and use them for competitions in sports without difficulty. They include the American Quarter Horse, Appaloosa, Tennessee Walker, Mustang as well as Cleveland bay are all examples of warmbloods.

If you're looking for quick-paced and energetic horses, look for breeds that are hot-blooded. They are commonly employed as horses for sports due to the level of power and agility they have. They can be difficult to manage as well as extremely temperamental. They prefer experienced owners. Examples of hot bloods include Arabian, Thoroughbred, and Morgan. They are commonly utilized in breeding systems to breed other horse breeds with distinct characteristics.

It is possible to look into the Hanoverian, American Saddlebred, Paint horse, Arabian and Morgan, in case you're looking for horses with grace and grace. These breeds sport a strong and well-defined body, and magnificent carriages and are great for riding pleasure.

Chapter 3: Behavioral Horse Training

Once you've mastered all of your physical training information in your head, it's time to look into the behavioral aspect of training.

A horse's acquisition does not immediately translate into riding immediately. Horses aren't vehicles that require to be controlled, without first establishing the relationship first. While riding, you must communicate with your horse in order to allow it to move faster, slower , and take turns. That means that both riders must be aware of the language they speak. Any miscommunication among the horses and rider could result in severe, if not painful accidents.

That's why it's essential to train your horse to be able to comprehend different commands, and thus make it possible for both of you as well as other riders to ride the horse without difficulties in communication or miscommunication. Training on the ground is the primary training method that is used to impart the fundamental behavioral understanding that each horse needs. There are many ground-based exercises that trainers use to help their horses gain a better understanding of basic instructions and scenarios.

Untrained horses are often scared of a variety of things in the world around them. This is why it is essential that the horse learn to live with the surrounding and remain in a calm state. It's no surprise that a horse who is scared could result in injury to the rider or trainer in the event that it is easily spooked by the normal elements of their surroundings. Another crucial thing to bear in mind is that, after basic training in behavioral and communication horses must be regularly taught to meet the demands of their respective fields of use. Dressage horses will be different in their behavior and communication training program since the horses will have to be trained to do various things.

In this article, we will examine different aspects of ground training and the routines used by trainers while conducting ground training for horses.

Ground training is typically used as the primary method of training to develop the manner of communication and behavior of horses in their early years. But, if older horses aren't adequately trained and have a lack of aspects of their behavior They are then exposed to the same type of training in order to help the horse comprehend these crucial lessons. For horses who are young the ground is an effective method of teaching the horse without putting the weight of the trainer/rider over its fragile body. The horse continues to grow physically and learn important cognitive lessons.

Longeing

This is a training technique that involves the motion of a hose with a green color in a circle , with the trainer situated in the middle in the center. The majority of the time, longeing involves the rope being that is held by the trainer, and later securing to the horse. It is also normal to observe trainers using a neither rope nor. The trainer is then able to guide the horse through the horse's body language, sound and gestures in addition to gentle tugging upon the rope. In logeing training the trainer uses several commands to get the horse to reduce its speed, increase it's pace, turn around, and so on.

Longeing is among the most significant training techniques that is used to improve the comprehension of body language in humans by horses. When performing these exercises, it is essential that the trainer avoid forcing the horse to run in one direction because it could become accustomed to this routine and not want to turn and run around in the reverse direction.

The practice of longeing is used to teach the young horse different elements of communicating. The exercises used in longeing are typically used to make horses familiar with various riding equipment, including reins and saddles. Longeing is also a great way to make a horse more familiar with its riding partner. The rider becomes comfortable with the horse within an environment that is controlled for safety reasons. It can also be used to train horses who are not suitable for riding.

Sacking

Sacking is among the most popular horse training methods that can trigger mixed reactions from trainers of different kinds. This method is used to de-sensitize the horse to things or elements that horses perceive to be terrifying. Horses that are not trained are typically scared of many aspects of modern life, such as the sound of music floating paper bags and even traffic. The most common reaction for horses when they're scared by things they find frightening is flight or fight. This can be extremely dangerous when it comes to riders. Horses are able to cause injuries to riders in situations of fear.

Sacking is intended to help familiarize the horse with the things that they find frightening. This helps horses remain calm in situations when they might otherwise be scared. The horse is taught to avoid the panicked reaction of fighting or fleeing and instead develop an interest to comprehend their environment and the frightening phenomenon.

In a typical sacking session, the trainer will bring something the horse would be frightened of. Let it be sniffed and then rub it onto the horse. This is intended to aid the horse in understanding that the object is safe. The trainer then lets the bag of paper go and observe what the horse does to it, now that it has become familiar with the item. The repeated exposure of the horse to such objects helps them to understand that there's nothing to fear.

While sacking can be beneficial to training horses but it is also disapproved of by a lot of trainers and is considered to be cruel and inhuman.

Liberty work

Liberty work is generally thought as a form of longing. In liberty work, the horse is taught how to respond to trainer's commands and body language throughout the entire time when riding or from the ground. The practice is carried out within a pen that is round, and there is no need for ropes to direct the horse. The freedom to freely move about the pen free of ropes is what is the reason for the name liberty work. Liberty work is thought of as an inherent horsemanship skill as the trainer seeks to understand the horse's needs and communicate with the horse.

Main Ground Training Objectives

In the course of ground training the trainer will make the horse more comfortable with human contact and interaction. It is crucial to remember that in order for a horse to be ridden you need to be able to touch it and get into close proximity with it. There are a variety of exercises that involve touching the horse over and over by scratching it, the introduction of it to an animal and tie it up to ensure it is accustomed to it are routine exercises. Ropes can also be introduced the horse, thrown on top of the horse or even on the horse's feet. These activities introduce horses to the routine of treatment.

Learning to read body language and other common human gestures is also an important lesson learned from ground-based training exercises. Trainers will attempt to get the horse to stop moving faster or slower and turn around with simple gestures. The primary gestures used here are the use of a finger to point or hand gestures as well as other gestures. The trainer's goal is to have the horse obey commands with no contact. This may involve the use of ropes in order to get the horse to walk towards or to the side of the teacher.

When you ride horses, you'll be confronted with a myriad of physical obstacles. It is essential to feel confident that your horse can do the necessary leaps, or, on the other hand, slow down and then move towards the obstruction. A horse, for instance, should be able side-pass along a fence or wall without misinterpreting the intention of the rider.

Normal riding also involves traveling through narrow areas. Training on the ground is intended to teach the horse to stay clear of rushing through narrow areas, thereby putting at risk the rider's life because of anxiety. The horse is taught to confidently move through these areas without fear.

Chapter 4: Global Horse Keeping And Riding

Preamble

Maintaining your horse's health is an chance that most people do not realize. You won't realize the importance of your horse until you're no longer able to have it. After having experienced some awful incidents at races for horses It would be nice to know that the handling of your horse and its usage could be given more focus.

It has been in the news since the beginning of time. The majority of the time the horses were viewed as an animal for the rich and there is a lot of sports activity involving the wealthy class of society, focusing on racing of horses.

This book focuses on providing a comprehensive overview on the condition of horse riding worldwide with a greater emphasis on the numerous areas in which the act of riding horses has always been highly regarded.

This ebook, which was prepared for our appreciated readers focuses on giving readers an in-depth understanding of the entire situation as it is the case with caring for horses, horse rearing and use.

Objectives

Horses are among the most noble companions that mankind has experienced ever had, since the time. Being in contact with a horse is not uncommon across all sections of society. In the past, and even in the near and distant past, the possession of horses was considered to be a sign of wealth, opulence and a status of well-to-do in society.

The most evident findings from the United States sadly note that the expense of keeping a horse for a long time exceeded the earnings of the majority of Americans each year. Therefore, it isn't economically viable in the event that your income is not enough to allow.

This is the reason why the realm of owning a horse has always been considered a private place that isn't frequented by the majority of people. The main reason that has always placed the use of horses ahead of the majority of people is the financial aspect and other risk involved with their use.

This book aims at exploring the various facets of the practice of rearing horses and use. The in-depth analysis of the study was essential to help people understand the various aspects involved in the life of the horse and the use of it. The ebook will also help to clarify the beliefs and practices that have been around for ages in relation to horse usage and the care of horses.

In examining horse racing as a form of sport and a form of entertainment, readers are expected to recognize the importance the horse has in the realm of leisure, as well as placing a high value on the animal when it comes to performing at the top levels of stamina and sportsmanship.

Terms of reference

The Book itself is a compilation of numerous research studies gathered from numerous sources on journals, the internet and interviews with horse owners from all over the world. A thorough analysis of the behavior of various horse breeds was conducted along with an analysis of money that are involved in the purchase as well as maintenance.

Recognizing that horses are costly to be kept for both pleasure and sport and for competition, the issues are expected to educate those involved on the immense job ahead following the acquisition of the horse.

The transition from traditional sports to the more exotic activities like horse racing has been an important aspect in the economic condition of many people around the world, whose earnings have increased dramatically.

The Book comes written in the form of a text that includes all financial representations interpreted in the form of estimates of their value to help the reader gain an accurate understanding of horsekeeping and usage.

Executive Summary

The entire procedure of horse keeping and its use within the racetrack as a game is among the major topics covered in this book. Because horses are an animal, diet is a crucial element in the growth of the animal and is crucial to clearly take into consideration the various aspects of a horse's diet as well as other supplements to help it maintain its vital endurance.

While the ownership of a horse can make for a thrilling experience, it can also lead to numerous challenges that the owner or the rider might encounter in certain instances which could result in fatal consequences to the pocket. This has made horse rental to be the most effective method to enjoy the stunning riding on horses.

Many people enjoy the simple appearance of horses, but not considering the many complex procedures that the owner of the horse might have had to go through to get the horse to a good place is a common occurrence.

The time taken to analyze the many different areas that define the use of horses globally is therefore an essential factor in having an opportunity to see the world from a different perspective of horse racing being accessible to everyone in every sphere of society.

It is the norm for a lot of people to utilize horses that aren't their own. The presence of a horse could be difficult if you're not a pro in the region. However, this requires training for both the horse as well as the owner, or even just the riding.

Similar to the story of the man who fell off the horse's back due to seeing a snake, something that could be avoided. We believed that examining these fascinating findings and compiling will not be wasted in the end.

1.0. Horse rearing

Looking after the young horse

Young horses are among the most difficult animals to take care of and might require some expert knowledge. The horse that is young must be fed with the appropriate types of food. The foal feeds that fall into this type of horse usually include large amounts of protein-rich feed that is accompanied by a serving of energy.

The horse should also be brought to the vet whenever experiencing tooth problems. It also demands that the hoof is regularly checked. Examining the social interactions of the foal, or foal as they are referred to, is crucial due to the fact that it is a part of rapid growth. Additionally, the caregiver must keep an eye the horse's behavior during education.

The training of a young horse is essential, particularly when it will be used for racing in sports.

Sometimes, the new horse can develop traits that are not beautiful. It is the job that a professional horseman has that the horse develops according to the correct way.

Check you have supplied with the proper housing, so that the foal is able to rest in the dark, and away from the elements.

The horse breeds that are common

Like the other wild animals in the world, horses can be just as different as their coloring suggests. There are a few specific breeds of breeds of horses which possess this characteristic to be used by the majority of horses. Some of the most notable horse breeds are:

The American saddle-bred horse is also known as the of the Kentucky saddler, is the cross breed of several of the most prestigious horses. It is famous for its ability to perform various gaits of horses, including trot. However, it's effective for its body thanks to its excellent physique and the ability to deliver very high-quality leaps.

Arabian horse- The Arabian horse is unique in its facial features that make it stand out. It is , however, a simple to connect with horses. Horses are willing and possess good stamina. They are ideal for those looking to utilize riding to heal. The colors are also different from black top brown.

Appaloosa horses- it is often referred to for its spotted appearance. It was the result of breeding Indian horses. They are generally gentle horses with have thin tails and manes. Their body is well-formed that allows them to jump and are popular in many horse races.

The American quarter horse is the most popular horse that is used in the majority of security activities. The reason for this is due to the versatility that the animal has. The horse can be utilized effectively by anyone who is new to the sport of horse riding. The horse is one of the most popular species in the world due to its rapid growth and can withstand almost any circumstance. The horse is strong body, which means they stable and have the speed to compete with.

It is the American paint horseis the most hardworking horse that is loved by cowboys due to their friendly nature. They come with two different coat markings that are distinctive.

The Peruvian Paso The Peruvian Paso Paso fino, the stunning horse is a breed of natural that has a distinctive gait, not common to other exotic breeds of horses. Because of its body form it one of the most easy riding horses. It is easy to handle and is naturally inclined, which means it doesn't require any training in order to ride.

The pinto horses are brown, and they are common sources of use when camouflage is required for a particular riding set-up. They are classified into four classes where ponies and horses are classified in different ways. They are referred to as saddlers as well as pleasure, sock or hunter based on the purpose of their usage. Pintos are a breed that is reserved and have been kept over the years.

Mustang horses- These are horses that are still primarily eating their bread naturally and can be found in areas that are preserved. They roam freely and are known to survive on their own. They are commonly called wild horses, but they might not be the best for anyone who is learning to ride. utilize.

The pony breed is smaller than the majority of horses pony are smaller. Most often, they can be obtained by interbreeding two ponies to create distinct breeds of horses. They are thus diverse based on the pony utilized in cross breeding. For example Connemara pony is one of them. Connemara pony is regarded for its ability to jump in a variety of riding sports.

Tennessee walking horse. This special horse is famous because of its trot. It doesn't trot but simply follows the rider along in strides that resemble walking. They are renowned for their walking but they can perform other gaits too. It horses is gentle that is exotic, and has a decent behavior. It has gained quite a bit of attention due to its usage, with the majority of them being used in ranches across the globe in certain instances as ceremonial animals to drive trails, which are accompanied by royalty.

The fundamentals of horse training

In addition to the other forms of requirements a horse might require before weaning the horse's training is typically focused on riding to ensure that the horse will be able to safely ride. Horses can be very agile, and the purpose of training is to regulate with the temperament of the animal. Horse training should be conducted by a trained professional who has worked with a variety of breeds of horses. Also, think about whether your horse is trained in different regions or is a new one.

The expectation of the horse plays a major role in ensuring the desired results are obtained. If, for instance, you're teaching your horse to jump, then the outcome must result in the fact that your horse is able to now jump at the highest level. Training horses requires faith and resiliency from the trainer when demonstrating to the horse how to do the desired thing.

The best way to go is find the most easy horse to handle in terms of temperament. This will be more secure than picking a temperamentally bad breed of horse. You can then follow a particular method of training to ensure uniformity. If it is possible, this has to be recorded.

Why is it so important to train your horse?

The horse's training is crucial in helping horses to reach certain milestones in life. The most crucial ions can be found in the following areas:

Trained horses are safer and have fewer accidents than horses who haven't been trained. They are able to coordinate their movements to the movements of the human body.

It helps give the horse survival instincts - horses that have been trained are aware and are able to recognize danger close by. This is a crucial aspect in helping both the horse and the rider be able to cope with threats such as the appearing of poisonous snakes.

Time savingsThe experience of riding a well-trained horse is more enjoyable and the horse does not have to spend much time at the track.

Commercial benefits: trained horses are champions at competitions of high-level races for horses. The rider receives enormous financial rewards at the conclusion of these competitions.

Are there risks to the rider if they are riding an untrained horse?

Each species has their own method of responding to the threat. The 'fight or fright' reacts to danger in one of those impulsive responses. A horse who is exposed to danger without any prior knowledge regarding the best way to approach confronting the danger could be unproductive for the horse.

Untrained horses can develop an isolation mindset, which might not be ideal for a social animal such as a horse.

The notion of class in the rearing of horses

The practice of raising horses is thought as a privilege for those with a lot of money in the society. Many horse breeding societies in Britain as well as in the United States contend to one fact : purchasing a horse and keeping it can be a significant expense. It is usually a process that requires one to meet a variety of prerequisites of having funding for food, housing as well as catering for the medical costs for the animal. In this regard, people of middle income have the money to buy a horse. The price is expected to be higher than the annual income of a middle-class household. For example, purchasing an animal could be priced about $3000. However , the cost of feeding each year could be more than the threshold of $5000.

This isn't an additional expense to the numerous other costs associated with vet visits and accommodation. For many, renting a horse is the only option for the rearing of horses left to society and government agencies as well as the wealthy of society.

1.1. The feed of the horse

The feed for horses is one of the most costly areas that horse owners be required to look after. Horses are fed with specific diets that range from hay to free grass for grazing, supplements as well as a range of food items.

What kind and amount of feed do the horse need?

Horses are fed a variety of diets, and they are dependent on different aspects of their age, the environment physical condition and overall health. In light of the above requirements, horses require specific amounts of feed, which is best determined by a specialist in horse care.

The feed for horses must contain a certain amount of protein in the form of crude energy , and vitamins. Horse feed is composed of such as maize, peas beans, oats Lucerne clover, wheat and perennial ryegrass, which form the phalaris grass, hay and other grasses that grow in pastures.

A 500kg horse's weight will require an average of 57MJME/kg feed daily of energy-rich feeds as well as 564g of protein, which is why it needs an average daily feed of 8kgs per day.

The key ingredients in the feed for horses

The feed for horses must include certain ingredients. They can be classified as well-balanced diet products. They can include:

Energy components

Crude proteins

Vitamins

Other mineral supplements

A well-balanced diet for the horse in the above meals allows it to be healthy and simultaneously, lets it to have the strength and endurance required for horse's use.

1.2. The horse housing

Horses are a popular and conservative animal that is popular and conservative. The reason isn't that the majority of people own it, however due to the huge costs that one needs to be aware of before acquiring one. The horseman should be able to have multiple homes with enough space to allow for the horse to roam freely.

Horses are essentially agile and should be kept to a secure area that they can't be expected to flee. If the horse is able to escape and cause damageto the property, the owner will be held accountable according to the case of Ryland vs. Fletcher (1868) legal law governing the liability of animals injured in tort.

The stable of the horse should be covered to shield the horse from extreme temperature and cold. The owner should make sure that the walls in the stabl.er are sturdy and durable enough to last for a long time. The walls could be made of wood or even just cement-based.

Horse housing is a must requirement whether you are looking to lease a horse to purchase. Many horse leasing companies make sure they have safe location for your horse.

What supplies do we need?

There aren't any restrictions regarding the materials used in the construction of the horse stable. Cement, wood, nails and iron sheets could suffice. But, depending on the financial status of the horseman, other elements that go into the stable construction could be required. The floor is poured with cement. allows people who clean to do it.

Chapter 5: Different Types Of Horse Training

The type of horsemanship that is used typically is related to the stage or age in the life of a horse. If a horse gets high-quality training at an early age it will be an excellent riding companion. Even wild horses can be trained to become calm and submissive.

Human Adaptation

Prior to any other thing the horse must receive the human acclimation program. This kind of training could be as easy as spending time with your new horse and grooming it properly. In this phase the horse is accustomed to humans. The horse eventually becomes at ease with his surroundings and new home. This type of training can last throughout the horse's lifetime.

There's a well-known method known as "Imprint Training" that is where handlers or trainers make contact within minutes following the birth of a baby. Humans can touch his entire body and talk to him and even touch his feet.

Another option is to let the foal be to its own devices for a couple of days or hours. In this period, the foal will form bonds with his dam or mother. It's important to take care of a foal when it is still nursing, and is not quite big enough to overwhelm humans. The foal will know that humans aren't going to hurt him, and humans are to be treated with respect.

The foals of the world aren't big enough and too young to ride however they are able to develop skills that will be crucial later on in their lives. When a foal is a year old, he must be halter-broke. This means that horses allow halters to be placed on its head. The foal should also learn when to stop if commanded or guided at a walk or trot, and also how to stand when tied.

Young horses must be groomed and looked after by a veterinarian in order to be dewormed and vaccinated. Horses must be calm and calm throughout these procedures. A regular hoof grooming is required so that a horse who is young must be able to follow the rules and stand as a farrier pulls his feet and cut the hoofs.

In this phase it is recommended that the foal learn the basic abilities he'll require throughout his lifetime. A few of these include being loaded in a trailer for horses being rescued in a field, and learning to not be scared of loud sounds. It is also normal for young horses to be exposed to sounds associated with normal human activities. They may encounter the sights of typical motor vehicles or the sounds of radio. In some cases, they're taught more advanced skills within their initial years, like peacefully allowing blankets to be put on them, and giving someone the ability to trim them using electric clippers, and not run when offered an opportunity to bathe with water from pipes. Foals also learn basic voice commands for stopping and starting.

There are also a few who choose not to deal with foals as often while they're nursing. Wait until the baby horse has weaned himself from his mother before he can begin halter breaking and other chores.

One method that is not widely used is to let young horses go untreated until they reach a point which they are safe to ride on. This is usually between two and four years old age. The horses are then able to complete the entire process of ground training and riding training. The drawback to this type of training horses is that it is more dangerous for humans, and trainers require a significant amount of experience to not get injured.

Ground Training

Training in the ground will happen throughout the life of a horse. It teaches horses to be able to move on leash without pulling or refusing to walk. Horses also learn respect at this point. There are two distinct disciplines that demonstrate the excellence of this kind of instruction such as showmanship, and halter. In the halter contest, judges rate those horses who have the best form. In showmanship, the horse shows the horse. Lunging and lunging are also part of ground training. Clicker training is also utilized here.

The young horse can't be being ridden, however, after the horse turns one years old, trainers generally introduce some ground-based training methods. The duration of this stage can vary from a few hours up to several months. All horses must be able to complete groundwork prior to being allowed to ride. While it's feasible to provide a small amount of groundwork for foals or yearlings, their bones as well as joints are less sturdy and are at the risk of injury. To reduce the risk of injury you should hold off until your horse has reached at least two years old.

Here are some of the most common techniques for ground training:

Longeing

This is the time to train horses to walk around in circles, while attached by a rope, which is usually between 25 and 30 feet long.

Liberty Work

It's also known as round penning, free-longeing also known as round pen work. This technique is where the handler is working an untrained horse with the pen of a small size, while the handler holds only the lariat of a long rope. The handler trains the horse to react to their facial expressions and vocal commands as they ask the horse to speed up and slow it down stop or shift directions.

Bitting

It is the procedure of getting horses to the bridle and bit. Most handlers include side harnesses, reins, or a surcingle to help them get the horse with the sensation of the pressure applied to the bit.

Desensitization

Also known as sacking out, desensitization is the process of getting a horse used to fluttering objects such as blankets, so that he allows himself to be brushed by objects similar to those. This helps a horse learn not to be scared of objects that move around him.

Ground Driving

This is also known as long-lining, and it allows a horse to move forward while the handler follows behind him. This happens prior to the harness is driven or used on the horse by a mount rider.

At this point horses may even be introduced harnesses or saddles without anyone stepping onto them or securing them to carts.

Before being ridden horses, they must be comfortable with the equipment that he will wear. The horse must be able to react to voice commands that are basic to stop, begin or change gaits and turn.

There are a few specific disciplines that utilize this technique to prepare horses to develop different forms of muscular. The drawback to this is that it blends both muscular and mental development , which means it could take longer than normal for the horse's readiness riding. The people who advocate this method advocate this because although it takes more time to complete groundwork and riding, horses advance faster once in the saddle.

Basic Training

Similar to the two initial stages of horse training, the basic level of training is also a part of the beginning in the life of a horse. The horse will not require this type of training in the future unless he was not properly trained initially. "Breaking" is a part of the basic training program to help teach the horse how to respect his horse's.

At this point the horse will be capable of walking, lope and trot at will. The ability to turn left and right is also taught. The horse will follow when he feels pressure on his legs and learns how to slow his pace or slow the speed of his movement. When you're teaching him with an equestrian discipline, your horse will be taught the ability to slow his pace, stop and then speed up.

It is also the time when the majority of horse breeds have been "backed". The distinction between breaking and backing is that the latter involves actually getting onto the back of the horse. The term "backing" doesn't mean the horse has to be ridden or moved on, it's just sitting on.

Breaking is the entire process of teaching horses how to be ridden. This means that horses are taught to remain calm and not get scared because of the rider's legs or actions. If this happens for the first time it is considered "green broken" however, after gaining experience and becoming more comfortable, he becomes an "well broken" horse.

The age at which the horse first gets being ridden or put in a saddle on is determined by the breed and discipline. The majority of stock horse breeds are first ridden by around the age of 2. A large number of Thoroughbred racehorses can be trained to take on smaller and lighter riders from the fall in their very first year. The horses that are employed in harness are typically taught to use carts behind them by the age of two years old. There are some horses who are taught to pull a lightweight cart although they're not allowed to ride until they reach the age of three. This helps them develop better manners and build more muscle mass.

A majority of the horses in all disciplines in the world are first introduced to riding when they turn three. The only exception is for breeds that take longer in maturing, so these aren't used until they reach four.

The aim is to make sure that horses be fearless of humans. They should view riding as an additional lesson to be learned. The horses that have done their training will rarely rear or buck or go away from the saddle.

Even horses who were never taught to ride are still able to learn. It may take longer because of their age, however it's still feasible. It's quite simple to train older horses so long as they're familiar with humans but do not possess any negative behavior. A wild horse that was rescued from the open field is extremely difficult to train. The most difficult horse to train can be a horse that is domesticated who has learned to disobey humans.

Western Discipline Training

There are numerous sub-categories of discipline training , and these will be discussed further. This stage can last for many years as the horse's handler trains and hones his skills. Western Discipline Training includes roping and team penning, reining trail riding, western pleasure pole bending, and the ranch horse.

English Discipline Training

The majority of trainers focus on English or Western discipline-based training. The former includes disciplines which include English pleasure and show jumping, dressage cross country, and endurance. Horse trainers can train a horse many subcategories.

Chapter 6: Socializing Your Horse

How to Train Your Horse to Allow It to Be

With everyone

Socializing your horse at an early age is vital. Are you aware of the reason? A horse that has a good socialization is not fearful or aggressive toward animals or humans. He is aware that people and dogs exist and aren't dangers to his security. A horse who is not socialized On the other hand believes that the world is in danger and responds with fear. He is scared and frightened when strangers or dogs appear. As soon as you take the Horse home, you have to begin socializing him. Introduce him to the presence of dogs and other humans within his world.

Attitude (Yours)

Your behavior is clear to your horse. He is able to read your thoughts like an author.

If you're upset with him, he'll feel the emotion. It is also possible to tell that you're having a bad day and will not be able to comprehend that your mood is nothing to be related to his. Thus, when you are in the process of socialization, it is important to keep a positive attitude and remain assertive. Your horse will be more bonded when he feels good impressions from you. Be patient, kind and encouraging. Be kind, caring, and affectionate.

Display more joy and pride than anger or anger or. If you are annoyed, take a break for a few minutes and take a deep breath and then try something new with your Horse and return when you are calm, cool and calm. Positive attitude is the key to success when you train your Horse. Do not keep pushing your Horse or being angry or you'll ruin the overall experience of training and performance for both of you.

The main purpose of the process of socializing your Horse is training your horse to be the type of horse you wish to see when you ride him later on. The Horse that he develops into is mostly formed during the beginning of his education. So, it is important to focus on the most important things during this time, and keep your eyes on the end objective. (The earlier you begin, the better the general rule of thumb for training.) Make a plan and stick to it and be consistent. Know what you are expecting from him , and communicate it clearly. You should be happy and thrilled when he accomplishes what you expect and praise him for his good behavior.

If you stick to these principles and follow these guidelines, you will be amazed by how effective you are in teaching with your brand new Horse. A major part of socializing is creating the unique bond you would like to share with your Horse throughout the course the time. It is important to do this by showing your horse how you're the herd leader. However, you must also demonstrate to him that you love your horse and that you are the best of buddies. If you follow the correct method as described in this guidance and behave towards your Horse as a true friend from the very beginning, he will be the most trustworthy and affectionate friend you've ever been able to have. Take your time socializing and show that you would like to be the best friend of this Horse however, you must demonstrate your horse that you're the most dominant leader and friend. Be gentle , but and firm. Give direction but not rude or aggressive. It is better to be firm than aggression when it comes to socializing the Horse.

How and when to socialize Your Horse

Your horse already started the process of socialization when he was just two hours old. In the meantime, he is socializing with his mother , and possibly some other horses when they are available. Of course, you can't simply think that the Horse to learn to be a competent horses to ride from their mother. The Horse should be exposed to humans and become accustomed to human contact at an early age. Because this is the most influential moment in the life of a horse and can really shape your horse as he grows. If your horse is older when you bring him into your life so don't fret about the effectiveness of your teaching him. You just have to put in a little more time with it. As soon as you have your Horse and you are able to begin handling him correctly as the Alpha. Moving his body and legs, stroke him, and converse with him. Make sure he is used to being treated by humans. Clean him every when you get off from his bathroom. He will be taught that you're not doing any harm, it's fun and will make him feel secured with his new herd-leader. Let your Horse experience a variety of situations. Ride him out for rides, walk to a trail with plenty of grass and other plants as well as a few other people wandering, exploring, and picnicking. Bring him on a trip to the shore, to a stream, a lake an aquisition or the local waterway. It's all in the details here. Take your time be creative and expose your child to a variety of landscapes that range from natural surroundings to trails and beaches. Based on the circumstances it could be necessary to walk along the gravel road to the trail, and could be in contact with cars that are moving slowly.

Trains, traffic, planes and even cars could be sounds that your horse hears. He will get used to the diverse surroundings and sounds that he's exposed to. If you're taking your Horse to various places it is possible to take him on the horse-trailer. This shows him that it's fine to be curious instead of being scared of all kinds of unfamiliar things. A truly Horse is a great horse.

If you are hosting friends invite them to meet your Horse so that he can get familiar with them and is able to be a friend to various people. It is important not to let him become too connected to you that he becomes distrustful of others. Spend time with your Horse and it will bind you two tightly. It also shows him the right way to behave and what's not acceptable when you interact with you and other people. It shows your child that you're a trustworthy, responsible owner who values your pet and that being with him means having fun, happy times. It's best to come up with a variety of physically and mentally stimulating exercises to keep him entertained and engaged. Important to allow your horse some alone time. This helps him to not be anxious when you're not around to connect with him. Place him in the pasture or paddock on his own for one hour or so several times throughout the day so that he can roam around. You can let him roam alone as well as with horses but not you.

Do not be afraid to correct your horse to avoid bad behaviors early. If he gets you nipped on the arm, say to him "No" strongly. Say "No" whenever he is fidgeting as he's brushed by the rail for hitching. If you start teaching him early about what is acceptable and what's not, the horse will become an obedient horse, and you'll need little or no corrections later on in the future.

Removing any negative behaviour and substituting it with a better one will let him know that you're the one in charge and he is required to pay attention to your every move. You'll be surprised by how much the man wants to be treated like this by you. Make sure he knows which actions are acceptable and what are not, beginning right now. Be firm, not abrasive.

Avoid physical punishments and shouting because these behaviors can make your horse suffer for the rest of his life. You do not want your horse to fear you, but instead to adore you with the utmost respect within his soul. All you need is a clear 'No' and a redirection to a different activity to modify a behavior disciplining your horse. It's now time to begin lightly training your horse. Of course, we will cover all of this in-depth throughout this book on horse training.

Introduce him to his Stall and Paddock and show the youngster that the stall is secure and safe that he can retreat to for peace and quiet , and also shelter from the elements. Do not use the paddock as a punishment or you'll see him hate the paddock and stay clear of it at all times. Soon, you'll realize that your Horse is a fan of his paddock and is adamant about the safety of grains, vitamins as well as fresh water, hay, and vitamins.

It is necessary to arrange an appointment with your veterinarian of choice to ensure that your Horse is up-to-date on vaccinations, worming, and worming and is in good health. Be sure to follow all the recommendations, such as feeding, training and exercise , and ask should there be any health issues.

Keep an eye on your horse's hooves and when they grow long, schedule an appointment with your reliable Farrier. Take note of all suggestions, even whether your horse has strong hooves or could benefit from shoes. There are some suggestions you can decide to follow.

Attitude (Yours)

Once your Horse is comfortable in his paddock, you will need to get him into serious training. This means that at this point you can train him within the pen in the round or with the long lead rope. We will discuss this in our next chapters. Make sure you take him on a walk to ensure that he is conditioned to the world that surrounds him. Introduce him to a broad array of horses, people and other places to help him over his fears and teach that he can take the world in the way it's. Socializing is a part of the horse's whole existence. You cannot lock him up in the paddock, and then expose him to strangers expecting him to behave comfortable around them whenever they come up again. Training and socializing your Horse is a lifetime journey. Every day, small steps will make a difference.

Fear Imprinting and the ability to overcome

Be aware that horses are subject to fear imprinting phase. Through these times, your horse could be prone to developing phobias. Every negative experience could leave a lasting impression on your horse's mind, creating the fear that will last throughout his life.

For instance your horse could be afraid of all people when a person is in a negative period. He could also be scared of children if a young one is constantly pulling at his back.

To prevent provoking fear in your horse, you should try not to expose him to things that scare him, such as the sound of fireworks on July 4th and yelling out in anger or causing unnecessary pain. Don't force him to behave in a rut in any moment of his life. Instead, be kind. Introduce him to noisy music, traffic and other common environment-related stimuli by taking him on regular strolls around the stables to help him to abandon the fearful mindset and teach him that the majority of stimuli are harmless. If you can expose him more to the world and the more relaxed of him he'll be.

Of course, some horses develop weird phobias. My horse was scared to leave the stables all by alone and without any other horses around him. I gradually allowed him to go to greater and greater distances every day. Every day I would make him go further and then let him stand for five minutes , then return. I would speak to him every time repeating, "Good boy, good boy Good boy." After about five minutes, we were enough that he couldn't more see any of the horses. He did not appear to be experiencing any anxiety about it, and we went on our one-hour excursion. He was never afraid of going out on his own. It took him a bag of sweets to overcome this one (for the two and us). The good thing is that we did manage to get plenty of fitness, so there's that.

For example the horse may be afraid to walk over a grass tarp. I'm not sure that he was worried that he'd slip, fall or slip or trip. However, whatever the reasons, the horse didn't wish to walk across the tarp. This was resolved by showing him another horse that was carried over the tarp. there was nothing wrong with the horse. The ears of the horse popped up, and he was at his eyes with awe. He then was able to follow the other horse across the tarp, and never again scared of it. Always make sure to say to him "good boy" every time you overcome a fear. Make him aware that what he's scared of won't harm him. Encourage him to develop positive, not negative ones.

If your horse is having a negative experience with someone or another horse, or another animal, it could make him nervous. However, this fear doesn't need to last forever If you are able to rectify it and help recondition the horse.

It is a good idea for him to be exposed to pleasant, pleasant, happy people including animals, and horses to demonstrate that not everyone is unabomber. For instance, if there is someone at the stables who was a screamer at your Horse you should be wary of the person due to obvious reasons. Let him meet other peaceful and calm individuals to help him overcome his fear of strangers. The ability to overcome fear is an essential element of socializing your Horse.

It is also possible to show him different aspects of you. Wear the hat or shave your beard, if you're an adult male with a beard. If you'd like to, that is, in addition, (I heard it grows in the back and gets thicker). It is possible to wear glasses, a dress or shorts, in lieu of jeans or slacks.

It is possible to change your hairstyle, apply an aftershave that smells different, or even shampoo. The person who is watching you will notice the changes. If you keep talking to him and tell him that everything is okay even if you look different He will come to accept that occasionally your appearance, or even your scent change. This will make him less anxious about changes.

Learn how you can take care of your new favorite pet.

Chapter 7: How Can I Improve My Trot Position?

It's not that difficult, is it? For most riders, the thought of getting your bottom smashed on the hordse4 once or twice frequently is not a possibility. Most of the time it is the habit for most riders to run trots. The best method to ride on a horse is to be in at a trot. A trot is usually either a rotational movement of your pelvis or rocking your hips as horses move. There are methods that have worked for many novice riders looking to learn to stand trot that could be worth trying. Follow the steps below:

Training-to ride a horse is a long-term commitment and so does learning to sit trot. The horse's rider has to lean in order to achieve the sitting right. Learning how to use the different saddles on horses can also be beneficial in this regard. For instance, with the English saddle it is lowered to 12 inches just by pushing the leather. This results in one stirrup going over the pommel and the other one is just in front of the pommel. In this way, the horse has a comfortable sitting position with their butts securely secured in the saddle. Although this can be difficult at first, as it makes the legs feel tight and you might need to align the hips and shoulders. It will result in an accurate sitting trot. It will require some practice, but in the end, you'll be in the correct sitting in a better position.

Learn the swayby sitting in the rear of the horse, and having it walk alongside you can also teach you how to sit trot. The most important aspect is mastering the skills gained through regular training. This will happen when you are able to walk the horse without stirrups. The trot's posturing is now simpler. But the key is to feel relaxed as the horse trots. It is normal for the muscles that surround the crotch region to be tight when riding.

How do you balance your horse during a jump?

The act of balancing your body on the horse is very crucial. The horse's movement should be in the same rhythm as your body moves is a skill that some may not possess.

Remember that when you ride, the horse is aware of your posture and will return the same way when you are riding rough it is likely that you will experience the same harshness and roughness back from your horse.

The method of making sure that your body is in a good balance is by allowing your muscles to relax. Many people, however, tend to make the opposite happen. The trick to getting a perfect balance is by practicing and learning the horse's posture such as trot postures.

Find the place that offers you the most peace of mind. The horse rider, in addition to ensuring that their seat safe enough for riding, must also master it without the need to grasp using either feet or knees.

It is not recommended to sit in the pelvis, as it will cause the butt to roll in every movement. Sitting on the three-point T seat, which is a combination of the pelvis and pubic bone might not be the ideal sitting position in the end. But, having both legs and the seat could aid in forming the ideal three seats for the horse since it can improve the movement on every jump.

A few tips could include making sure the face is held up and straight to keep away from distractions. Additionally, the stirrups could be reduced in the event that the horse is within the edge of a jump to ensure balance of the body mass of the rider. If the location that the ride is taking place is dangerous, make sure that the rider wears head straps to maintain balance and to prevent the risk of tipping over.

Which is an intermediary horse riding definition?

The horse riding experience is comprised of various unique gaits that every professional horse rider must be able to manage efficiently. A horse rider who is intermediate is a horse rider who can successfully manage all gaits involved when riding a horse without difficulties. But, an intermediate rider may not be typically a complete professional, he's not a beginner and can navigate his horse without assistance.

The rider must be conscious of the horse's mood and shifts in their movement at any point in moment. A rider who is intermediate in this regard is an expert rider, and is distinct from an inexperienced rider.

When a novice horse rider is still in the learning process and could be at risk, an intermediate horse riders are believed to be able to discern risks at any time.

What can I do to stop fast horses?

There are various methods used by people to stop a horse that is speeding. The most popular techniques are those that use convection. They are employed by most people in the case of an emergency while riding. Horses have different training and understanding the way they react could make a difference when it gets too fast. If you hold and pulling on the reins. the ride is often instances stopped in the event of danger.

What do horseback riders require?

It's not far from the truth. All horses require a full set of equipment for riding horses. The horse's owner may restrict certain things based on their requirements. But, there are some things that should be kept in the clothing closets of all horse rider.

The clothing includes helmets as well as gloves, riding pant boots, and a fit saddle for horses. The saddle assists as the rider sits on the horse and helps keep the horse in a perfect position. To secure the saddle into place, the rider might require a girth or cinch.

In areas with high risk of danger it is possible for the rider to wear a breastplate, or a breast collar to ensure that the saddle is in a safe place. pads are essential for comfort and safety of riders. There are a few things the horse's rider might require to put on the horse, such as the noseband and curb chain, for example, aids in managing the horse. Additionally, bits are important to a horse rider , based upon the degree of professionalism that one has achieved.

Chapter 8: Horse Stall And Paddock

It is preferential if you keep your horse in a horse stall that has an enclosed paddock. Technically speaking, it's not a horse stall, but more appropriately referred to as the horse shelter. A stall usually measures at minimum 12x12 feet and is sealed on all four sides with the door shut to keep the horse inside at least for the duration of. A horse shelter is shut on three sides. The fourth wall is left open to ensure that horses can leave or enter anytime.

The shelter could include an access door that allows you for bringing your horse into or out, and to feed your horse twice each day. My shelters are equipped with an open half door that splits so that you can keep the top of the door open, more like an opening for your horse to look out frequently. The top opening also allows access to feed. The top door is closed at night , when the weather is predicted to be difficult.

I am able to access the hay rack on the right of the door , and the grain feeder can be found to the side of the shelter's the bottom door. So I can put an occasional flake of hay into the rack and then dump the grain in a small bucket into his feeder, without opening the door at the bottom. One horse needs an hay bag in order to minimize the amount of hay he throws upon the floor. The bag can be accessed via the front windows to facilitate feeding.

The shelters measure 12x12 feet in dimensions. The paddocks need to be at minimum 25x50 feet or more. If you don't have an animal property and you is boarding the horse in an establishment or small stables and stables, you might have to look around for the ideal conditions for your horse's life. We don't recommend a stall that is turned out every day unless you want to be an exhibit horse.

If you choose to purchase a full-time pasture horse we would recommend that your horse be kept in a place to shelter in the area. If you own your Horse in your property, then you'll have to scoop the manure in the paddocks regularly. It is possible to employ a professional to clean your paddocks or make minor repairs to your property. If you're cleaning your paddocks by yourself, we suggest that you do it regularly or at the very least every two days. The reason behind this is that the more frequently you clean it, the less work you have to do which means your horse's going to be able to have less parasites and flies to deal with.

I've cleaned paddocks during the winter, with snow falling after seven days. Each paddock had an entire wheel barrel of manure. If the weather isn't conducive to cleaning, you'll face an immense task to complete. This is the reason we suggest regular cleaning as often as is you can. Manure should be kept in a manure container until it is converted into fertilizer. The fertilizer is spread out over your pastures, or you could sell it at $10.00 per load. It is also a great option to use for gardens. If you have stables for horses or a horse farm, you could purchase or lease a tractor that has front-end loader and mower. The tractor can be used to mow your pastures at minimum every two years when grasses start to grow. You can utilize the front-end loader to stir the manure pile every month.

It is possible to use the front end loader for spreading fertilizer every two years. It is also possible to use an harrow to spread manure around the pasture. These are just a few benefits that come with boarding your horse at the nearby stable. It is easy to pay monthly fees for the board. The owner of the stable is responsible for feeding manure, cleaning, purchasing an implement and tractor and regular farm work.

Additionally, there is a clause in the agreement that states the owner will immediately notify you when health issues arise. Also, you should provide the stable owner with the number to contact your Vet in the event of an emergency. If you have only one horse and the price for your region is $400 to $500, it's an excellent value. Plus, you get more time for close contact with your new friend!

The reason why a horse stall and paddock are the best for horses

A paddock and stall for horses typically work well for horses. With an stall for horses and a paddock horses can go in or out at any time. He has more freedom, even though he's inside the paddock for the duration of the night. You'll have total control over the time that you let your Horse out and when you let him in. In late spring and the beginning of summer, you'll enjoy the best growth period for grass.

As we mentioned previously as mentioned earlier, As mentioned previously, a Horse may fall over due to excessive sugar content in the grass. The founder could turn into laminitis which can end up killing your Horse. The affected horse is most likely to be killed and it can be an extremely painful experience.

In the peak growth season when we are at our highest growth, we leave our horses out for about 3 hours each day. In the winter, autumn and spring months, we see lots of rain. The rain pools up and the grass isn't suitable for horses. We limit grazing to about 1-2 hours a day, and on certain days we do not allow horses out for any length of time.

On other days, if the weather is right they can be out for 10 hours or more. The main reasons I allow them to go out, if it is possible is that they're getting exercise throughout the time they are out grazing and they are eating around one pound grass each hour. If they're outside for 10 hours, I will only have to feed them around 10 % of their hay each night. It's an all-win scenario.

Your horse always prefers fresh pasture grass instead of the hay and will always prefer to exercise and graze. The horse that is grazing throughout the day, will walk about 8 miles a day grazing. Also, you can will save money on costs for hay. Your horse is likely to consume 7300 pounds of hay or grass every year. If you bought the three string bales for 100 pounds, and gave him hay with no grass for pasture the total would be the equivalent of 65 bales per horse. It is possible to purchase a semi-trailer of hay every year for a reasonable cost per bale. It is also possible to purchase bales separately, 10-20 bales at the same time.

We pay around $23.00 per bale of 3-string Orchard Grass here at my site. With that amount, hay itself costs more than $100.00 in a month per horse. Vitamins are 30 % of a month for each horse. The vitamins bags are 50 pounds, and will last a horse for 50 days for $23.00 in a bag. The COB (corn or oats), as well as barley) is much more affordable priced at $12.00 to 50 pounds. A single bag of COB could keep a horse fed for approximately one month.

Horse treats come in 20-pound bags . One bag is enough for one horse to last around

3 months for $12.00 for each bag. As you can see , the costs increase when your horse spends less time in the grass. There are many benefits to having your horse boarding. However, regardless of what you choose to do about boarding, boarding, or having the property of a horse and a paddock that has a shelter and a daily time for pasture is the one you and your horse would like best.

Take a couple of days for your Horse to become accustomed to being on the Stall. When you transport your Horse to the new place it's going to appear as a strange space for him. The majority of Horses like to have a friend in the pasture. Another horse within the paddock that is connected will give your horse an animal companion who can be able to share the pasture with during turnout time. Stalls are usually separated but are connected. In the evening, no horse will be lonely since they often listen to each other's breathing and snort or whine within the stall that is connected.

Once your horse has become accustomed to his new pasture companion and paddock for about 2-3 days, it's the perfect time to start creating a bond and your pet. On the first day, just put on the horse's halter and give him a thorough brush. Take him for a walk before returning him to his paddock. On the second day, you can do the same thing and then saddle him up and put on the bridle. Then, you can walk him around for a while. Every day you spend time with him you will gradually increase the amount of time you spend with him. Don't attempt to ride the horse for more than one week of warm-up activities.

Selecting the perfect Living Space for your Horse

We've discussed a lot of this in the past however it is essential to create the perfect habitat and home that your horse can thrive in. We've covered the reasons the reasons to place your horses in paddocks, with shelter and a companion to keep him entertained while he's out on the grass almost every day.

If you own the property of your horse You will have more control over your horse's wellbeing. If you plan to board your Horse You may need choose the right place however, it might not be the perfect one. You might not have many choices to pick from. There could be only a few stables near your residence. You could bring the Horse to one place and then a month later transfer to the second one because of numerous reasons. Care feed and a pasture companion as well as your capacity to talk with the owner of the stable, and shelter should be taken into account.

If you're Horse are "Alpha" Horse and the pasture buddy can also be an Alpha you could transfer him to a new area because of being a battle between the horses. If you're taking a boarding position, it is vital to have a fair relationship with the owner of the stable. Do not be afraid to suggest he locate another horse with whom your horse can be with. If a more suitable pasture companion is found, you won't have to move your Horse back. A lot of moves at once can be stressful for an untrained Horse.

Where do you board Your Horse

If you do not have an animal property, you'll have no alternatives than to take care of your Horse. It is common for the owner of a horse will choose to purchase another horse, and then later the third. If you're boarding your horse and paying for it, financial concerns become an issue. If you're paying between $1000.00 or at least $1500.00 per month for the cost of boarding, and you pay $1200.00 per month in rental or a mortgage payment then you might want to think about purchasing a smaller horse stable as well as you to live in instead of staying in boarding. If you study and discover that the mortgage cost for a horse ranch of 5 acres and a three-bedroom house is about $1900.00 If you do, you could think about it as less expensive than the cost of boarding. You'll even have enough cash to cover feed and some other costs for maintenance. Don't forget to take into account the time needed to maintain the ranch. If you work 40 hours per week , and are able to spend 20 hours each week, your time is likely to be slowed by general maintenance of your ranch. The extra time will usually take up time you would have spent with your horses.

Setting up the stall

There aren't many furniture in a barn or stall. They're usually filled with hard-packed dirt and gravel that can make your horse uncomfortable on his feet. The shelter is usually fitted with stall mats that give an inch of padding. The mats for stalls are made of made of rubber and are typically sizes of 4x6 feet. The majority of shelter floors are covered by six mats. The shelter must also be equipped with an hay rack that can keep the majority all hay from building over the floor. Certain horses can cause a mess with the hay, especially if it's stored inside a rack. These horses might require a haybag to lessen how much hay is that is wasted in the dirt. The net-like bag will help reduce the amount hay lying on the floor. They'll eat only the hay that is on the floor until it is dirty, wet, dirty manure, or pee on it. If the hay becomes dirty, it has to be removed. You can reuse the hay in a small way by filling an area that is muddy or to create a Puddle. A hay bag can aid in reducing wasted hay for specific horses. It can also be helpful to have an animal feeder in order to reduce the waste of grain. The hay rack and grain feeder should be set in such a manner that your horse will feed without having to go into his stall every time. This is the same when using a hay bag. It is possible to hang the hay bag on the stall's hooks that clip on to the ring that is placed within the door. It's an excellent idea to provide horse troughs that are pure, fresh water that is shared between two horses that share the paddocks. The shelters for the horses might require some repairs if a hurricane causes a shingle to fall off or paint begins to peel. Horses may enjoy playing with a big ball that is tied to ropes inside his stall. All horses need a salt-based lick inside the shelter. This is the size of your shelter or stall.

Start Your Relationship!

As we mentioned before Every interaction and activity you engage in to do with your Horse is about developing your relationship. Talk with your Horse frequently during every interaction and contact. Share your thoughts and observations regarding every interaction. Make sure to hug him every day in the neck area for a minimum of 30 seconds. Put your face in the neck of his and smell his scent. Put your chest against his. He might be shocked the first time you perform this. He might try to get away from you for a few times. Do not let him go once the person steps back. Move forward with him and hold him for 30 seconds. In no time, your horse begins to take pleasure in your hugs too. You can give him commands, while talking to him whenever required. When you put on your harness and begin to lead him out of the stall, you should say "Walk" and ensure that he follows you when he walks through the stall's door. If you tie him up on the rail of hitching to groom him, you should repeat, "Stand," then you can say, "Good Boy," whenever he behaves as you instructed him to do.

Properly handled

Safety is the main concern when you handle your Horse. It is my opinion that if you are not confident in how to ride and handle the horse, you'll require a few lessons prior to taking part in these book's instructions. It is possible that you will need to learn how to put on a halter saddle , and bridle. It is important to know how to take each hoof, and then employ a hoof pick to scrub the hoof's bottom thoroughly. You must know how to tie your horse to let him away from the stall each day you work together. It is important to be attentive when dealing with your Horse. If a dog chases and frightens your Horse He could react in a dangerous way. He might attempt to sprint, kick or even stand up to defend himself. If you're not ready and alert it is possible to be dragged, kicked , or even trampled. A Horse may cause death to a person after becoming agitated. To prevent such a scenario it is possible to clear the way, or take off his lead rope to ensure that you are secure. It's helpful to speak to your Horse frequently in a peaceful, calm tone. This can help prevent your horse from reacting quickly when he's scared.

Your horse will not learn to be scared by too many different stimuli. He'll likely become accustomed to being a dog. If you have to walk past an entire herd of Llamas while walking along a trail you can be a bit shocked when he has never seen this sort species of creature before. The animal may stop and stare for a few seconds, then look up with each exhale. Be calm and calm with him as you gently stroke his neck. Let him know that they're not going to harm him in the future. Remind him that he's an excellent boy. Squeeze his ribs by bending your legs and say "Walk," then calmly walk along. When you have walked three times through the Llamas, he will probably not react the next time. It is important to talk to your Horse continuously and calmly. As you handle your Horse you will be able to confront and overcome his fears in a short time If you're always to calm his fears.

Chapter 9: Understanding Your Horse

Horses are highly smart They're also habit animals that are able to adapt well to routines This means that by perseverance, they'll be able to learn quickly as they respond to repeated routines and strategies.

They respond most when they're bonded with their trainer, a horse needs to trust its rider to be able to accomplish any goal in the training process, therefore building a connection to your animal is the first and foremost.

Like us, horses are also individuals, and you need to know what your horse feel, is it a shy horse that requires care and attention? Are you a bold and unruly hose that requires some discipline and resiliency? Or is it an attentive horse, willing to follow the rules?

It is essential to know the information before you start your instruction.

The process of establishing a connection can be accomplished by a variety of methods, however the easiest one is to be initiated by bodily contact. Whether it's with whips, hands, spurs or even a saddle.

It is important to know what soothes and irritates your horse.

With this knowledge You just need to know that a horse is to comfort or trying to avoid discomfort. A horse that is well-trained will concentrate any training on creating a comfortable environment and comfortable for his horse.

In the event that a horse has been put against discomfort, its response is not positive and it can range from being unresponsive to straight fear.

Horses are the fast-moving animals they are due to the fact that they have created a strong defense against danger. in the scenario of "Fight or flight" they'll most likely choose flight, because they evolved to be speedy.

Keep that in mind as you learn about your horse's how it is comfortable or uncomfortable will be, and you'll have the essential information you need for training it!

Connecting with Your Horse

When you train horses, the primary objective is to have an organized, controlled and intelligent horse and although the methods employed to train horses vary, they all will require you to communicate with your horse and for that, you have to be based on the same fundamentals which include:

* Basic Control

* Lightness

* *

* Line

* Connection

To be a successful horseman, it is essential to undergo the intense training process and usually, it's a task to lead and connect horses who are challenged. This art is passed from generation to generation and you shouldn't let that bring you down!

One of the best ways to begin learning and interacting with your horse is to spend time practicing commands such as "Go" as well as the "Stop" commands. Another phrase you should become comfortable by can be "cue".

A cue is essentially an indication of pressure, you can use them to control your horse. Another control methods are body movements because horses - being intelligent animalslearn to connect with the commands you give them.

If you are establishing an underlying language for cueing for your horse you must to maintain it within the triple Cs of cueing, constant, clear and concise. If you don't, it can lead to your horse going back to its normal instinct, and thus acting in fear.

If you're feeling like you've run into a roadblock for your horse, take some time to review your cueing language. It can be a huge help to your horse.

Cueing Your Horse

To teach your horse to be a better horse, it is important to focus on your cues consistently, patiently and above all, positively You may be asking yourself what exactly does this mean I'll help you understand the pillars of training.

"Constantly" refers to the fact that whenever applying pressure on your horse you apply pressure continuously and in a manner that, once it has moved in the right direction, you let go of the pressure. In this allows your horse to understand what it is he must do to avoid the pressure and then starts to follow you with any trouble.

"Patiently" is the term used to describe when you train horses, that you conduct the training in a manner that is calm and keep your distance and making sure that the message is across. You repeat the message several times and praise it.

"Positively" indicates that you have positive attitudes, having an unattractive attitude or being a bit frightened can only stress your horse, which can make him anxious or nervous which isn't any difference to you or your horse.

Keep in mind that a horse will only learn when calm, and being stressed isn't good for the horse!

Chapter 10: Fight Or Flight

Every horse, regardless of how well-trained they are have an instinctual "fight and flight" instinct that is built into their brains. It's essential to survival. When in the wild, when the herd is threatened by a predator and the herd is threatened, it's the responsibility of all horses to alert each other of the danger and it's the responsibility of the leader horse to guide the herd towards safe. When you or your horse are into a frightening situation (even the situation isn't necessarily frightening to you, but that is unfamiliar and potentially dangerous to the horse, like a loud plastic bag along the trail, or a gunshot in the vicinity) you must remain in control the horse's foot. In the event of an emergency it is essential for your horse to trust you and to listen to your instructions. If you can teach to your horses that you're the leading horse, they will be able to follow you and will trust you, even in most frightening circumstances.

Flight or fight can't be derived from horses. If you're looking for horses, you'll frequently hear phrases such as "dead broken" to convince that the horse cannot be scared. Although many horses are "desensitized" to items that normally make a horse nervous (like gunshots and plastic bags) there are times that a horse is scared because it's the nature of nature , and that's the way the species has been able to endure for the longest time. Many people take every effort to keep their horse safe and try to stay clear of frightening situations. This isn't good for the horse, it's making it harder for them to learn (this issue is explained in the next few pages).

How to Avoid Being the Lead Horse

Horses like to be educated, they would like to remain in a state that is comfortable. When the horse is genetically bound to have one lead horse in any herd, they don't wish to be the leading horse. They want to feel at ease knowing that a different horse is responsible for taking care of them.

The most effective method of "train" the horse to do it through the use of pain. Horses aren't responsive to the pain of others. If you really desire to establish a relationship to your horse and show to them that you're a the leader horse, don't employ whips, spurs, chains, bits or any other means to achieve this. In the pages to follow shear dynamics are explained in easy details to help you trigger your horse's instincts naturally and teach them to behave in a manner that is genuine horsemanship.

The pain is a shortcut

Most people aren't aware of how uncomfortable the "tools" we utilize every day really are. For instance, spurs (sharp metal pieces that are attached to heels on boots) aren't training horses to move whenever they are kicked. A little (the metal piece inside their mouth) doesn't teach the horse to go to a specific place by pulling at the reins. Whips do not teach your horse to run after they struck. Everything that a horse does has to be based on the release and pressure. It is the easiest way to get rid of pain. There are many trainers who take the horse for thirty 60, 90, or 90 days, then take your money and won't even be able to work with their horses. If you've ever been advised by a trainer you'll not be able visit your horse in that time (no regardless of your reason) or "just require a few more days/weeks/months" choose an alternative trainer.

A skilled trainer will help you in educating your horse. Many people believe that sending their horse away for a period of one, two or three months can "fix" the issue. Even if your trainer has done an excellent job and can demonstrate the lessons they've given your horse but if you're not aware of how to properly guide your horse after you have brought your animal back there's a great possibility that the issues from before are likely to recur.

The horses don't require any training, it's the riders who do. Horses will do whatever that you ask them to do, all you need to be able to ask them.

"If you receive the wrong answer, then you've asked the wrong question."

"Rick Gore," horse trainer

Pressure and Release

The most important aspect of horsemanship is knowing the difference between pressure and release. When you know how to apply pressure to your horse, and also how to allow them to release then you'll be able to teach any horse. However, to utilize pressure and release correctly you need to recognize these signs.

Here are some instances of release and pressure:

Pressure: You squeeze the left rein to cause the horse turning.

Release Once your horse begins to take on the pressure and is willing to do the thing you request, release the tension by loosening the reins.

Pressure: You press their hind end with a stick to make them go away.

Let go: When you release your horse, it is moving their hind leg to free themselves from the pressure. So you release the stick and let your body relax.

"Horses take their lessons from pressure release, and not from the actual pressure."

Missy Wryn, trainer of horses

Body Language

Body language is a vital element communication with your horse. Horses communicate through the entire human body. A tail that is active can mean an animal that is agitated, however, it could also mean that they're throwing flies at them. Moving their feet may indicate anger, or they may kick their stomachs to ward off bugs. A pinned ear could signal the horse below to get away from them, or could indicate aggression.

Understanding your horse's language requires many years of experience. You must be aware of the fundamentals of horse communication generally, but you should also get to understand your horse. Every horse has a distinct personality that is their own. being able to get to know them by being in their presence and watching them around the farm will allow you to understand your horse better and enable you to give them more guidance.

Ear, Tail, and Body

If your horse's ears are straight back and flat against their necks It's an indication of aggression and something you need to be attentive to. Horses may pin their ears against an animal (to cause them to get away) or even at you and tell the person that you've did harm to them, or that they do not want you to be near them, etc.

Pining your ear is often an indication that is given prior to an attack or kick.

If you are listening to your voice horses may be watching you from the side of his eyes and his ears remain at a comfortable position. If you're riding and the horse's ears are in a relaxed position and pointing back at you, they're focusing on your signals.

If a horse is aware of something that is threatening, or is watching another horse, they'll raise their head (to see more clearly) and their ears pointing forward. This is the sign of alertness and they're likely to enter the flight mode.

If the horse is about get into fighting mode it will appear bigger. They'll bow their necks and ears inwards or pin on their head, and their neck will be raised.

Be aware of your horse's behavior as they sleep or relax. Check their ear positions to be aware of how your horse appears while they're sleeping, relaxed, paying attention to your voice, or when they're alert, etc. The act of watching your horse is the most effective method of learning their language.

Be on the lookout for your horse's feet and tails. If they're relaxed, they'll often rest their back legs by lifting their weight off of it and resting it on the tip of the hoof. This can be easily misinterpreted by new owners of horses. A horse can do something similar to this when they're getting ready to kick. Check your horse's entire body to determine if it's relaxed or are about to kick something. If the horse's head appears in a low position it's likely they're in a state of relaxation. If the head's up and/or the ears are forward, there's a high chance that they're going to kick.

If you are you are working with your horse, it is best to work in a secure area, free of other people and horses. If you happen to be near your horse, and they pull their ears or leave it is important to look over the situation immediately before fixing your horse. Was a horse higher than them inform them to get off? This can happen. It doesn't matter how high or low your horse's position within the group, human beings are more powerful than horses. If you're staying at a stable, or have several horses and horses, you must teach each member of your herd. Whatever the height of the horse right next to you the horse must pay attention to you and not.

Don't let Horses Teach You. Horse Teach You

Horses are the greatest teachers of horses. If you're not doing things right they'll let you know by not performing what you request. A clear direction and a thorough understanding of your horse is vital to creating a bond and ensuring that your horse is aware of what you're looking for. Horses don't like being beaten, and they'll never attempt to provoke you into anger. If your horse isn't responding to one signal then you must change the way you're acting.

"Insanity is repeating the same repeated thing over and over and expecting different outcomes." ~Albert Einstein

If one method isn't working Try a different approach. The most important thing is to don't get angry with your horse. Be patient and consistent are the new friends you'll have working with horses. You'll be able to create an ongoing relationship if your horse has confidence that they can trust you. It's fine to discipline your horse and you shouldn't be afraid to correct them in the event that they do something to your or kick at you, etc. They are risky actions and your horse should be aware of what it is not allowed to do in the presence of humans. The reason for these rules is to safeguard the horse. If a horse discovers that they can kick, bite and rear up when people manage them, they'll get called "dangerous" and then dismissed or neglected. If you're teaching your horse these kinds of rules and rules, they'll be able to enjoy a peaceful and secure existence in the world of humans. A proper training program means that your horse knows the things you want them do and not allowed to do, however we don't correct them through aggression and anger. Do not act in a way that is impulsive with horses.

Correcting Your Horse

Prior to correcting your horse's behavior, you should ask you three of the following questions

1. Did I provide clear instructions regarding what I wanted them to accomplish?

2. Are I acting because of emotion (frustration or anger, fear and so on.)?

3. Was the way they did it potentially dangerous (kicking at you or cutting you)?

If the answer to the 3rd answer is yes then you must always take your horse to the right place and be aware of if you're acting in a state of emotional turmoil regardless of the circumstances. When we're emotional we aren't able to provide precise direction and aren't able to see the whole picture of the circumstances. Determining the best way to correct your horse's behavior needs to be planned ahead of time. If you're working with a horse the first time and you're going to tie them up and lead them, or to lead them round the pen and so on. Be sure to know what you'll do if they yell at you or bite you and charge you, etc. Why? because you must correct the situation in which it occurred and not wait for three days, or two minutes after the incident. They will not be able to connect the dots.

Here are some suggestions of how to correct your horse's behavior:

They bite you If you're on floor with the horses (leading them, or standing beside them) and you get bitten, immediately alter your posture, say "no" with a firm voice and then take them away. A horse that is backed up displays power.

"He who puts his feet first, is the one in charge."

Missy Wryn, trainer for horses

If you "change your posture," you must maintain an aggressive, dominant posture. Horses communicate via their bodies and even though using the word "no" can be a way to strengthen your correction and your body will be involved with it. Get up straight, stand tall, gaze at your horse and speak with a firm voice. Be assertive and forceful, not hostile. Begin walking towards your horse, and get them to move. If you're behind them, get them to come back using a shaking of your lead, telling them "back" or moving toward them. They must leave. If they don't, then you have to increase the tension until they will. This can be accomplished by slinging a rope close to their location (but refraining from hitting them) and then moving it towards them.

If your horse doesn't move away from the pressure, you're not stern enough. Do not simply walk away and forget about it. Your horse must be aware that you are able to be able to move around (because you're the leader horse) and that they are not able to bite you. When your horse is off from your side, let them go. the pressure.

They will kick you It is usually not understood and some horse owners who aren't experienced become very scared even when they don't have to be. This is where reading your horse's entire gait is helpful. Most of the time when you request canter (above trot, or below the gallop) horses will raise or rear when they change gaits.

Before you correct, you need be asking yourself "are they trying to hit me?"

If you're riding a horse around and you tell for them to get off and they kick when they go away, they're probably kicking to get into the canter or are annoyed. However when your horse is kicking at you when you're on the ground but they're not moving away, it's time to correct the situation.

Making your horse move his feet is the most effective way in order to "correct" your horse's. Horses do not like moving or doing things they don't need to. When you force them to move their feet, you're accomplishing two things:

1. By moving their feet, they show them that you're in charge

2. If you force a horse to work when they're doing the wrong thing it makes the right choice simple

If you're persistent enough, the horse will discover that if they do not listen to you, or kicking or biting. You'll need to do their work. Soon, the horse may be accepting cooperation instead of being forced to run.

Chapter 11: Horse Breeding

If you own horses among the most important things you'll need be aware of is reproduction. While certain aspects of the process of reproduction are dependent on the veterinarian that is attending however, the success of a breeding operation is largely dependent on your knowledge and control in the course of operation.

Horse reproduction is designed to produce healthy and healthy foals following each successful mating. It is a complex process that leads to the birth of a foal, and the success of the breeding phase is contingent on the understanding you have of your stallion's and mare's reproduction capabilities. In this section we'll go over some important aspects of horse breeding and reproduction that you're required to know as a horse's owner. While it is possible to get a vet handle or guide you through some of the processes for reproduction however, it's more beneficial if you possess the knowledge essential for successful breeding of horses. This will assist you in making the right decisions and obtain the most effective outcomes.

Horse Selection

The most vital aspects of breeding horses is selecting a breeder horse. In general, this is one of the most important aspects that determine the outcome that the breeder can achieve. Chances of getting an energised and healthy foal also depends on the selection process of your horse.

It is essential to know the progeny data of your horses, since this can help you identify the top breeding horses. Your veterinarian can help in selecting the most healthy mare and stallion to breed. If this is done correctly the breeding process will likely yield more positive results, leading to a pregnancy that is successful and an unharmed foal.

It is the Examen of the Reproductive Examination of the Mare

The need for a reproductive examination is to determine the state of reproduction that your horse is in. The procedure includes rectal palpation as well as ultrasound examination. When you undergo a reproductive exam, the vagina, cervix and the vestibule are examined by your veterinarian to determine if the mare is in a normal reproductive state.

Reproductive tests are best conducted in a stall, or at the entryway to the stall, rather than an open area. This keeps the horse contained and gives some level of security to the vet and the other personnel who are handling the horse. If your horse is pregnant or has foals, they must not be separated since this could cause the mare anxious and create a difficult exam. Apart from having the horse in a secure manner and secured, it is beneficial to have another person on hand to help the vet.

To stop the spread of illness between mares to prevent the spread of disease, disposable equipment must be employed. The mare needs to be cleaned to eliminate the fecal matter and dirt that has accumulated in the vulva prior to exam. If you are having an ultrasound exam it is best to do it in a dark, shaded area away from the sun to ensure that the vet is able to read the display of the ultrasound device.

Learning about The mare's Estrous Cycle of the Mare

As with all animals, a horse is subject to an annual cycle of fertility as a result of fluctuations of hormone levels. The cycle of reproduction is complete in around 21 days. For horses, the reproduction cycle occurs in two stages. It is an ongoing cycle in that the mare's in the heat (or during the season) usually lasting around 5 - 7 days. Also, there is the dioestrus period, which is the time between successive heat spells, lasting between 14 and 16 days).

In mares that are not pregnant the estrous cycle is generally stimulated by the increase in daylight hours. Therefore, it is associated with the beginning of spring. There is typically an in-between phase that can last for a few weeks, and may be marked by irregular, short cycles. But, following the first cycle of ovulation, the estrous cycle will be more stable and regular up to the fall and then the mare will begin an anoestrous cycle after which ovulation ceases.

Changes in hormones within the horse trigger an estrous cycle. The hormones released during different stages of the cycle include prostaglandin, progesterone (PG) and estrogen, luteinizing hormone and Follicle-stimulating Hormone (FSH). Production of these hormones is a factor in the course through the estrous process and some are required for maintaining the pregnancy.

Mare Management

The breeding process in horses is inefficient when compared to breeding in other domestic animals. In general, 50 percent of the mares at an stud will never have a baby. This is a terribly inefficient and inefficient procedure. One of the factors that could affect the effectiveness of horse breeding is the poor selection process for mares to be used to breed. As a breeder you should be aware of the potential causes and the factors that cause the waste of breeding horses and then work to eliminate these.

An accurate assessment of mare fertility is crucial for successful breeding. This procedure is utilized to determine if a horse is suitable to be used in service. A fertility assessment can help to determine the causes that could cause a decrease in fertility. It will assess mares and then place their ranking in order according to the likelihood of successful breeding process.

A proper fertility test will ensure that the mare is only served during an estrous time, as this will give it a greater chances of conception. After each breeding season, a thorough veterinary inspections and examinations must be carried out on your mares. Mares who fail to conceive should be examined and issues identified and addressed prior to the beginning of the next breeding season.

Stallion Management

The management of a stallion is largely on the purpose it is being kept. Stallions may be trained for racing, for show or even for breeding. This will decide how the stallion will be handled regarding handling exercising, health care and most importantly, fertility evaluation.

If you intend to raise your stallion for breedingpurposes, you must have a good understanding of how the reproduction system works is necessary. A stallion's reproductive system is comprised of the scrotum, tests penis, testes glands, epididymis and the spermatic cord. The organs have to be in good health to be a stallion being trained to breed.

Horse Teasing

One of the primary phases of breeding horses is the process of teasing. It is nearly impossible for your horse to think of a new idea without an effective teasing system. The success of this method is dependent on how you are able to determine if your mare is pregnant and will respond to stallion services. Typically, when the breeding season begins the stallion has a small period of between 5 and 7 days during the 21-day month cycle. The remaining 14-16 day period of your estrous cycle is non-concept days when conception is not likely.

Some mares might display signs of the "on" season even in the absence of male horses The majority of mares have to be stimulated by a stallion colt before showing they are hot. Teasing can be performed in a variety of methods. However, regardless of the method used you should employ a flexible and methodical approach because each mare is distinct and the same method is not applicable to all mares.

The signs that indicate it is an estrous time include:

Accepting the teaser

The lifting of the tail

Urinating

Wink

Squatting

If a horse isn't sexually active, it will display the following indicators:

Rejection of teaser

The teaser is kicked off

Removing the ears

Clamping her tail down

Interfering with the Horse Breeding Process

Sometimes human involvement might be necessary to gain control and increase the likelihood of success for a breeder's program for horses. This may take the form of hormone therapy or Artificial lighting systems.

Hormone Therapy

Hormone production is among the most important factors that affect the process of breeding horses. Hormone therapy is typically used as a method to manipulate barren or maiden mares in order to increase their odds of conception. Females who are pregnant can undergo hormone therapy. If done properly the hormone therapy could improve the reproduction capabilities of your horse significantly.

Keep a record Keeping

Another crucial aspect of a successful horse breeding program is keeping records. A complete and thorough document of the horses you have can play significant part in helping you to make informed decisions about the potential of breeding. In addition to the progeny records of each mare and stud You should also keep a tracker of teasing of all your mares and make it available to your veterinarian for a fertility evaluation.

Artificial Lighting Programs

The role of light plays an important part within the cycle of estrous for horses. The time of the beginning of breeding seasons is usually defined by longer durations of sunshine. So, a well-designed artificial lighting program could improve performances of horses as the breeding cycle is affected by daylight hours. By extending the duration of daylight with artificial light sources, mares will be enticed into the season earlier than they typically do. Artificial lighting is also able to boost the efficiency of pregnant mares.

Laboratory Aids to Enhance Reproductive Performance

In addition to simple fertility tests and tests, a variety of tests in the laboratory can be conducted to determine the horse's fertility as well as diagnose issues and address medical problems. The tests that can be conducted include bacteriological exams as well as biopsy, cytology, hormone tests and endoscopic tests.

Serving the Mare

Once you have a grasp of the fundamental principles of breeding horses as well as the elements that affect the effectiveness of a breeding program You can begin mating the horses. Keep in mind that the success at this phase is contingent on the efficacy of your selection procedure and the horse's ability to tame itself. The four main methods of getting your mare to have a foal include paddock service, hand mating and artificial fertilization or embryo transfer.

Weaning and Foaling

After a mare is successfully conceived the pregnancy can last for about 330- 342 days. You need to be able to identify the pregnancy early. This ensures that you don't return pregnant mares for service. It is possible to diagnose pregnancy by hand, with an ultrasonic exam, or through testing in the laboratory.

A pregnant mare requires high quality medical care as it will significantly affect whether the pregnancy is carried to term, and also how healthy the baby that is born. A basic treatment plan for an expectant mare can include:

The provision of forage that is nutritious

Reduce the exposure of other horses in order to decrease the chance of injury and illness

Deworming and vaccination

A veterinarian can provide additional care.

Do not transport your mare during the pregnancy unless absolutely essential.

Twin conception is usually a challenge for mares. This is the reason the early detection of pregnancy is crucial. A ultrasound test is required approximately 14 to 16 days after ovulation and the embryo should be removed in order in order to let the other grow normally.

Preliminary Signs Of A Birth

The typical pregnancy lasts approximately 330-342 days. When the time comes for birth the horizon, and there are indications to be aware of which indicate that a birth is coming soon. The time frame of these indicators varies depending on the mare the next be prepared for a imminent birth. The most noticeable and reliable signs to be on the lookout for are:

The filling in the udder (occurs between 2 and 4 weeks before foaling)

Teats are stretched out (this happens between 4 and six days before foaling)

The teats are waxed (occurs from 1 to 4 days prior to foaling)

Milky drippings that are obvious

An increase in the calcium content of milk (this is detectable with a the test kit for stalls)

Other subtle signs include a vulva that is relaxed as well as changes in the position of the foal and weakening of the croup muscles.

It's difficult to pinpoint the exact date of foaling. But, in the last phase of gestation the mare is likely to exhibit indicators of labor. The signs to look for at the start of labor are:

Unrest

Moving up and going down

Curling of the lip at the top

The shift in weight and the lifting of the hind legs

Frequent urination & defecation

The tail sways

Foaling

If a mare is about to give birth, it can be beneficial having an attendant present. Most of the time the mare will receive just a bit or none help. However, it is advantageous to have someone on ready to help should it be needed.

At birth, the chorioallantois ruptures and the baby begins in the pelvic canal. The baby should have two forelegs and its nose resting on its. Uteri and abdominal contractions are likely to force it out. This will take between 10 and 20 minutes.

In general, the mare will be able to give birth to her foal with no assistance. If help is provided, it needs to be provided in the form of holding gently the foal's feet as the horse is allowed to move independently. A vet's attention is only required when there is an abnormal appearance or behavior of the foal.

Care for the Newborn Foal

After 30 minutes from birth A healthy foal will be capable of standing on its own after a few unsuccessful attempts. Once stable it will search for the mare's teats and feed. It's not a perfect process however, with a little help from the mare and foal, it will locate the teat, and will suckle on in a natural way.

Below are the typical behaviors that should be observed during the first 2 hours following the birth of a foal:

Foal breathes (immediately following the birth)

Heads up (within 5 minutes)

Begin to stand up in 10 minutes, and do it in 55 mins.

Voice (within 15 minutes)

Defecates (within 30 minutes)

Suckles (Within one hour)

Begins with a walk or run (within 30 minutes)

Have an afternoon sleep (within of 3 hours)

Understanding the normal behavior of foals is vital to identify possible problems and seeking help when you require it.

In the initial few weeks after birth, the baby will nurse frequently, with approximately three or two sessions per hour. As time passes, the length and frequency of nursing will be reduced, and they consume different feedstuffs more. The foal will stay close to the dam for its first couple of weeks, but will slowly move out into the world around it.

After the birth of foals, the first thing to do is check that the foal breathing. Go to the area of foaling to determine whether the foal's breathing is normal and then remove the birth bag from the foal's skull If you have to. After you've verified it is breathing the foal, you can say your task is complete in the present. You should leave the foaling area and observe only from an extended distance.

If the foal's breathing isn't independently then you can gently make its nostrils tingle with grass or straw, or blow it into the mouth of the foal. If none of the above methods work, rub and shake it vigorously. press its ribs with a gentle squeeze or lift its head off of the floor and then dropping it.

Cut the umbilical cord right away following birth. Instead allow foals or mares to cut it when they move. After the cord has broken it, you can put 1 to 2% of mild Iodine to the stump to help it dry out and stop the spread of a bacterial infection that could cause severe illnesses or even death in foals. Be sure to monitor the naval stump for a couple of days to make sure it's closed. If it does not, contact an animal vet.

Typically, the foal should be in a position to stand independently within an hour of birth. Initial attempts might fail however, with time the foal will eventually get habit of standing and get more steady after a few days. It is best to let the foal stand on its own, since lifting it up onto its feet prior to being fully prepared could cause strain on ligaments and tendons.

The foal will instinctively look to find the udder in less than one hour after birth. It is an exploratory procedure that may take time for the foal's to get used to. Avoid the urge to intervene since this could impact the bond between the mare as well as foal. Interventions are required only when the foal hasn't nursed in the two hours following the birth or if it appears your mare refusing the foal's attempts to nurse.

Help the foal gently get up on its feet and then guide it towards its udder. Sometimes, a horse with an udder that is swelling or a young mare that is not experienced and has sensitive teats need to be controlled before she willfully allows an infant to feed. In extreme situations it is possible for the mare to be calmed by a veterinarian if she continues to refuse the foal's attempts to nurse.

Colostrum

The initial form of fluid that is produced by the mare right following the birth is referred to as the colostrum. The milk is full of antibodies to protect against disease and also other essential nutrients. It is therefore essential for your foal to receive colostrum shortly after birth. The ability of the foal to absorb these important antibodies will decrease significantly after 12 hours after birth. Make sure that you allow your newborn to nurse from his mother in the first 12 hours.

You can boost the amount of antibodies in the colostrum of the mare by vaccination about 30 days prior to the birth of the foal. If this isn't done the first time, you must give the foal a tetanus vaccination upon birth. This will safeguard the foal for approximately 2 to 3 weeks, while the umbilical stump is healed.

Colostrum is also a laxative as well as helping foals to eliminate the excrement from the fetus (also called meconium) within a short time after having it (usually within 4 hours). Constipation can occur if the foal is unable to be able to bowelize within the specified time.

Chapter 12: A Different Method To Get Your Horse Into The Trailer

Since there isn't a right or wrong method to train horses, you may want to change the method you use for training your horse. There are alternatives to choose from. If you're having trouble using a particular method You can always try another.

Here's another method of teaching your horse how to get into the trailer.

The first thing that you must be able to communicate with both your horse and yourself. It is crucial for your horse to understand the tasks you want for him to do and it is important to allow your horse to understand what you would like him to accomplish.

Once the horse becomes proficient at walking in both directions at this moment, it's time to connect the lead rope to the halter and then lunge the horse from side to side. If, for instance, you make a left-handed gesture you want the horse to turn to your left. At when you point to the right, you want the horse to go to the opposite side.

The end result is likely to be like this. You're carrying the lead rope as you ride your horse. As you carry the rope in the right thumb, you're going to tie the lead rope into the left hand. The rope should be raised until the horse can be aware of it, and aim towards the left.

Because your horse knows what he needs to do then he'll immediately turn to the left. After a few circles and then you'll change hands, and the same motions is going allow your horse to turn towards your left.

When your horse has mastered that, let him pass through the gate and barn door entry and on. You'll want to make use of smaller places to push the horse through, giving him with the opportunity to overcome his natural fear of being claustrophobic. It is possible to accomplish this by luring your pet between yourself and the hedge. When he goes between sides to side, you can make the space between the fence and you less. Make sure you don't get trampled.

When he's realized that, you will be in a position to lead him through the trailer. Lock the door to the trailer and allow the horse a chance to sniff the scent. Then , you'll return, and when meeting your horse, you will sway towards the right and left just in front of the trailer as you see him moving back and forth in the doorway.

After all the person who is guiding and sending your horse is aware of the message you intend to convey. You've communicated to him that when you point to the right, the horse will move to the left and so on.

The next step to be to force him to look at the trailer. When his head is facing the trailer, and you to his left, you will at this point, point and then send him directly to the back of the truck. Certain horses will jump right into the trailer, whereas others may require more effort.

If your horse doesn't want to go into the trailer after you have been pointing and encouraging him, get your horse away from the trailer and let him task. Now you're communicating the notion that being in the trailer is a sign that the horse is able to relax. Being out of the trailer suggests that he must do his best. At some point, he'll begin to learn.

After you have him inside the trailer, it is important to give him a pat and let him unwind. It is important for him to see how fantastic it was, so you can talk to him.

Horse Making Loading Mistakes

1. The idea that your horse looks like either a cat or dog.

If the new owner of the horse is aware that they are a horse, they may think their horse looks like an animal or cat. The horse's new owner could raise his thigh and shout "C'mon" a few times, and the horse may just stomp into the trailer like the dog were happy.

2. Food as a bait

Another mistake they often make is to place fruit, hay, grains, or other foods on the front of the trailer to tempt the horse to eat the food. It's almost never successful. If it did however, it could be the best thing to happen. Certain horses will be able to lean on and attempt to get food. But, they won't go into the trailer if their lives were in danger.

3rd error: Not realizing that the trailer needs to be connected to the truck

A few horse owners who are new will fail attaching the trailer to their truck before attempting to place the horse inside the trailer. If the trailer is not connected and the horse stepping into the trailer, it will move. This is likely make the horse nervous and make it more difficult to keep him in the trailer again.

4. Starting an "Tug-o-War" on your horse

There are some who will try to pull the rope of lead to pull their horse inside the trailer. This is then transformed into a standard game called "tug-o-war." So, which one do you think will win either you or the pound-for-pound animal. The loading of a horse into the trailer is not easy However, using these strategies could cause irritation or cause injury.

5th Mistake Beginning on the trail before the horse has become proficient in getting into the trailer.

Many horse owners will to bring their horse inside the trailer for a brief moment and then assume that the training is over. Therefore, when they decide to ride on trails the horse won't be able to be able to return inside the trailer. The reason behind this is that they were not able to practice leaving and entering the trailer enough to embed it into the horse's head.

It seems like there's always that moment when a horse owner doesn't be able to get their horse in the trailer. One of the ways to overcome this is communicate with the horse how to communicate to ensure that the horse likely to comprehend the actions you would like to accomplish. A portion of this is related to the way that the person and horse communicate.

Conclusion

Horses are extremely athletic that require lots of training to bring them into their peak condition and maximize their full potential. It is crucial to have a good understanding of information about horse training in the event that you decide to purchase an untrained horse to make sure you provide it with the proper attention to keep it physically and mentally well-trained. If you are conducting horse training that is physical, you'll find that your horse is subject to various injury risk based on the amount of training that is put on it. The trick is not as much to be aware of the different types of exercises to be conducted but to have an understanding of how to recognize the impact that the exercises take to the horse. This will assist the trainer choose the most appropriate training balance to keep the horse healthy and reduce the chance of injury.

However prior to any physical exercises are conducted by a horse, it is crucial to tone the horse's behavior and understand its communication. The purpose of this training is to enhance the connection between the horse with its environment as well as with people. The behavioral training of the horse provides it with the knowledge necessary for knowing the basic commands that are that are used by trainers and riders in their directing. In the end, horses have been known to follow the instructions of their leader on the move.

Be it physical or behavioral the horse's training is crucial to ensure the health of any domestic horse.

www.ingramcontent.com/pod-product-compliance
Lightning Source LLC
Chambersburg PA
CBHW071838080526
44589CB00012B/1033